LOVE ONE ANOTHER

40 DAILY REFLECTIONS FROM THE LETTERS OF 1, 2, AND 3 JOHN

40-DAY BIBLE STUDY SERIES
BOOK 9

PETER DEHAAN

Library of Congress Control Number: 9798888090077

Published by Rock Rooster Books, Grand Rapids, Michigan

ISBN:

- 979-8-88809-006-0 (e-book)
- 979-8-88809-007-7 (paperback)
- 979-8-88809-008-4 (hardcover)
- 979-8-88809-040-4 (audiobook)

Credits:

- Developmental editor: Julie Harbison
- Copy editor: Robyn Mulder
- Cover design: Taryn Nergaard
- Author photo: Chelsie Jensen Photography

To Dan DeHaan

Series by Peter DeHaan

40-Day Bible Study Series takes a fresh and practical look into Scripture, book by book.

Bible Character Sketches Series celebrates people in Scripture, from the well-known to the obscure.

Holiday Celebration Bible Study Series rejoices in the holidays with Jesus.

Visiting Churches Series takes an in-person look at church practices and traditions to inform and inspire today's followers of Jesus.

Be the first to hear about Peter's new books and receive updates at PeterDeHaan.com/updates.

CONTENTS

JOHN'S LETTERS

The apostle John (not to be confused with John the Baptist) is one of Jesus's twelve disciples and part of Jesus's inner circle, along with his older brother James and his friend Peter. But there's more. In his biography of Jesus, John refers to himself as the disciple Jesus loved.

Imagine that.

Consider that Jesus has many followers. He picks twelve of them to be his disciples and three of them to be in his inner circle, but beyond that John rises above them all as the disciple Jesus loves. (The word *love* occurs often in John's writing, which we'll cover throughout this book.)

John also wrote five of the New Testament books. Only Paul wrote more.

As far as the New Testament's content, John wrote about 20 percent of it. Only Paul and Luke wrote more, about 33 percent and 25 percent respectively. This clearly places John as one of the top three authors in the New Testament and a leading source of our Scriptural understanding of Jesus and our faith.

It's interesting that Paul wrote only letters (epistles), while Luke wrote only historical accounts (the books of Luke and Acts). John, however, wrote in both of these genres, as well as a prophetic book, making his contributions to the Bible more holistic.

John is best known for his beloved biography of Jesus (his historical book). Many cite it as their favorite gospel for its poetic language and unique content.

John is also well known for his epic vision of the end times, called Revelation (his prophetic book). Its evocative imagery intrigues and perplexes readers.

John's three letters—1 John, 2 John, and 3 John —however, are not as well known. This is unfortunate as they present valuable insights to help us grow in our faith and understanding of what it means to follow Jesus. This is most true of his longest letter, 1 John.

We'll dig deep into these three letters to mine

simple truths and profound insights to move us forward on our faith journey.

[Discover more about John's writing in *Living Water: 40 Reflections on Jesus's Life and Love from the Gospel of John* and *A New Heaven and a New Earth: 40 Practical Insights from John's Book of Revelation.*]

JOHN'S FIRST LETTER

Some refer to the book of John as the gospel of love because he mentions the word *love* thirty-nine times, more than Matthew, Mark, and Luke combined and more than any other book in the New Testament. In all the Bible, only the lengthy 150-chapter book of Psalms uses *love* more often.

In John's much shorter letter of 1 John, *love* shows up twenty-seven times (and seven more times in 2 and 3 John). John, it seems, is all about love. And as followers of Jesus, so should we. That is, we should love one another. This is what Jesus tells us to do and what John repeats to us.

Unlike most of the letters in the New Testament, John doesn't address 1 John to a specific church or person, with content unique to them. Instead, he gives universal truths for everyone. As such, we can apply 1 John to ourselves to follow Jesus with more intention and greater confidence.

How well do we do at loving others? What can we do to love more fully?

[Discover more about love in John 3:16, John 13:34–35, and 1 Corinthians 13.]

DAY 1: WORD OF LIFE
1 JOHN 1:1

This we proclaim concerning the Word of life. (1 John 1:1)

We notice many similarities between the beginning verses of 1 John and the opening passage of the gospel of John. We don't know which one John wrote first, but we sense that one informed the other. It could be that John wrote his letter first and then expanded on the opening verses when he wrote his biography of Jesus. Or it could be the other way around, with John penning his gospel first and condensing the first eighteen verses to begin his letter.

In the opening lines of 1 John, the disciple confirms Jesus's presence at our world's formation (also consider John 1:1–2). And John confirms Jesus's presence during the apostle's lifetime.

Consider other biblical writers. We can applaud Luke for investigating the life of Jesus to write his biography of the Messiah (Luke 1:3–4). We can also affirm Paul's experience with Jesus who appeared to him last (1 Corinthians 15:7–8) in a supernatural encounter (Acts 9:3–6).

Yet John reminds us that his knowledge of Jesus is firsthand. He has an eyewitness account of the life of Jesus. Using the pronoun *we*, John says he's not alone in his testimony of the Messiah. It was a group encounter.

Along with others, John heard Jesus's words. John saw Jesus with his own eyes. And after Jesus rose from the dead, John experienced the resurrected Christ, looking at him and seeing his scars (John 20:20).

John writes his letter to tell others of his experience with the Savior. He proclaims what he knows about the Word of life—about Jesus—to his readers then and to us today.

In addition to being the Messiah (the Christ) and our Savior, Jesus is the Word of life.

Just as the words he spoke brought forth life during creation, the words he spoke during his time on earth brought forth life to those who followed him then—and to us now. And when we die, the Word of life will bring forth eternal life for us so we can join him and live with him in paradise.

Yes, Jesus is the Word of life.

And John proclaims the Word of life to the readers of his letter so that we can personally experience Jesus. His kingdom is for us now *and* for eternity. As the Word of life, he guides us in how to live our lives today and guides us into living with him forever.

If we hear Jesus's words and believe in him, we will have eternal life (John 5:24). Do you believe in the Word of life?

[Discover more about the Word of life in Philippians 2:16 and the words of eternal life in John 6:68.]

DAY 2: FELLOWSHIP
1 JOHN 1:2–3

We proclaim to you what we have seen and heard, so that you also may have fellowship with us. (1 John 1:3)

Building on the phrase *Word of life*, John continues by saying that the life appeared —that is, Jesus appeared—whom John has seen and testifies about. He proclaims Jesus's life (eternal life) to us.

Why does he do this? He doesn't say it's so we'll go to heaven when we die, even though eternal life is a sweet outcome of following Jesus.

John's goal is that we might enjoy fellowship with other followers of Jesus. And this fellowship is also with Father God and his Son. This means that as part of Jesus's church, we can also fellowship with our Creator and our Savior.

But *fellowship* is a strange word to me.

As a child, the only time I ever heard *fellowship* was when churches had "fellowship hour" or "a time of fellowship." This meant the adults would sit around drinking coffee, making small talk, and laughing at amusing anecdotes. Aside from taking place in a church building, God had little part in our fellowship time.

But *fellowship* bored us kids. For our part, we spent *fellowship time* seeking creative ways to entertain ourselves, with the goal of avoiding getting into trouble.

Though supplying some insight, the dictionary doesn't offer much clarity into what John means with *fellowship* either. In defining *fellowship*, it talks about companionship, friendship, and comradeship. This understanding may explain most churches' fellowship time, but it falls short of what Christian fellowship could and should be.

The churches' and the dictionary's superficial views of *fellowship* aren't what John writes about. The reality that God is part of our *fellowship* suggests it exists, at least in part, on a spiritual level where we enjoy a supernatural connection.

Consider the pair of disciples walking to Emmaus after Jesus's crucifixion. The resurrected Christ appears to them, but they don't recognize him. When they at last realize who he is, Jesus disappears. Reflecting on what happened, they say, "Weren't our hearts burning when he talked to us and explained the Scriptures?" (Luke 24:32).

Having our hearts burn within us is an example of fellowship.

God-honoring fellowship should cause our hearts to burn when we talk about the things of God, explore the Bible together, and live in authentic Christian community.

And we can also experience this intense, personal fellowship with God. Through the Holy Spirit, we can connect with God the Father and God the Son in the spiritual realm.

This fellowship with other believers and with our Lord is why John proclaims Jesus. And when we follow Jesus, we can experience this sincere, profound, and deep connection on a spiritual level.

Is our fellowship sitting around drinking coffee or is there more to it? How can we have fellowship with God?

[Discover more about fellowship in Acts 2:42, 1 Corinthians 1:9, and 2 Corinthians 13:14, as well as 1 John 1:6–7.]

DAY 3: COMPLETE JOY
1 JOHN 1:4

We write this to make our joy complete. (1 John 1:4)

John uses the pronoun *we* a lot in this letter, over forty times in its short five chapters. Later we'll see him use *we* as inclusive language to embrace all those who follow Jesus. Yet other times, especially in the opening, *we* refers to himself and a group of unidentified others who join him in penning this epistle.

John now says that their purpose in writing is to make their joy complete. On the surface it strikes me as a self-centered reason. It's as if he's not writing for our benefit, but for his, quite simply to experience complete joy.

Yet when we're doing what God calls us to do, joy should be the outcome. As we obey him fully, it's reasonable to expect that we'll have complete joy.

The word *joy* appears in over half of the books of the Bible. John uses it in all three of his letters, as well as in his biography of Jesus.

Joy is more than happiness. Some people are often happy, but they're not as often joyful. We can think of joy as an immense satisfaction or an intense, ecstatic happiness. We can experience joy in an accomplishment or in a situation.

For example, I feel joy each time I complete a book to share with others. It's an outcome of being obedient and answering God's call to do my part to advance his kingdom. Whether it's few people or many—I pray that it's many—I know that my words will affect others on their journey with Jesus. This fills me with joy.

Even more so, joy fills me knowing that my books are a legacy. They can continue to encourage others in the future, even after I move from this earth to live with Jesus eternally. This gives me even more joy. I might say it makes my joy complete.

In addition to accomplishments, situations can also fill me with joy.

These seldom occur when I'm alone. They

happen when I'm with others, enjoying community with them. It's times of Christian fellowship—the kind John writes about—that fill me with joy.

In this way, fellowship and joy connect, with God-honoring fellowship producing God-given joy.

Another situation that fills me with joy doesn't occur when I'm savoring a spiritual connection with people. Instead, it's when I'm connecting with God. Though I need to be in the company of others to interact with them, I can interact with the Almighty at any time.

Sitting with him and basking in his presence in the spiritual realm fills me with joy, an indescribable joy. In fact, I had a time of fellowship with him as I sought his direction on what to write for this chapter. And the results fill me with joy.

If our fellowship doesn't produce joy, what needs to change? How can we make our joy complete?

[Discover more about joy in 2 John 1:4 and 12. Read what Jesus says about joy in John 15:11, John 16:19–24, and John 17:13.]

BONUS CONTENT: PARALLELS BETWEEN JOHN AND 1 JOHN

This is the message we have heard from him and declare to you: God is light. (1 John 1:5)

The opening to John's gospel and John's first letter share many striking similarities, with recurring phrases appearing in both. Here are the key ones that jump out in the first chapter, reminding us of the beautiful alignment between these two books.

- The beginning (John 1:1 and 1 John 1:1)
- The Word (John 1:1 and 1 John 1:1)
- Life (John 1:4 and 1 John 1:1–2)
- Light (John 1:4–9 and 1 John 1:5–7)

- Darkness (John 1:5 and 1 John 1:5–6)
- Truth (John 1:14, 17 and 1 John 1:6, 8)

Elsewhere in 1 John, other recurring themes that are also in John pop up as well. These include love, sin, the need to believe, and eternal life. We'll cover these in the days ahead.

What does the consistency between these two books tell us? How can we apply these examples to use Scripture to inform Scripture when we study the Bible?

[Discover more about the value of God's word in John 5:39–40 and 2 Timothy 3:16–17.]

DAY 4: GOD IS LIGHT
1 JOHN 1:5–7

God is light; in him there is no darkness at all. (1 John 1:5)

As John continues in his letter, he moves from fellowship and joy, to talking about the light. God is light. That is, the Father, Son, and Holy Spirit give us light. In their light there is no darkness. The good light of Jesus overcomes the darkness of the enemy where sin and evil abound.

John discusses this light—the light that shines in the darkness—in depth in his biography of Jesus (John 1:4–9). It's a great parallel passage to today's reading, with the two smartly complementing each other. But there's more.

Let's go back to the beginning, back to creation. Jesus is at creation, and all created things come through him (John 1:2–3). When creating our reality, God first makes light. He declares that this light is good. He separates light from darkness. This marks the first day of creation (Genesis 1:3–5).

Not only is Jesus—who gives light and is light— present at creation, he'll also be present at the end of the age. This is when God ushers in a new heaven and a new earth.

This new heaven and new earth will contain a new Jerusalem. This city will not need sun or moon to illuminate it, for God will light it through the lamp of the Lamb, the light of Jesus. All nations and their rulers will walk by this light and give their glory to it—that is, to Jesus, the light (Revelation 21:23–24).

From their thrones in the great city, God the Father and Jesus the Lamb will rule. They'll give light to all, without the need for sun or lamps. In the light of our Lord there will be no more night, with God's light forever chasing away darkness (Revelation 22:5).

Throughout this we see Jesus as light: at creation, during his time on earth, and for all eternity. And, as followers of him, he is our light today.

The light of Jesus pushes away all darkness.

Now John ties this back to fellowship. If we claim to have fellowship with our Lord yet continue to walk in darkness—that is, in sin—we delude ourselves. But if we walk in his light, we'll enjoy fellowship with other believers because Jesus has purified us from all sin.

We may worry that our sinful actions remove us from fellowship and make us liars. But we must remember that as followers of Jesus he has forgiven our sins (Hebrews 8:12 and 1 John 1:9; see Day 5). This includes both in the past and for the future. As a result, we're qualified to experience fellowship with one another and with God.

Thank you, Jesus!

Have we received the light of Jesus? How can we fully embrace the truth that when Jesus died for our sins, he has forgiven them and remembers them no more?

[Discover more about light and darkness in John 3:19–21, John 8:12, and 1 John 2:8–11.]

DAY 5: CONFESS OUR SINS
1 JOHN 1:8–10

If we confess our sins, he is faithful and just and will forgive us our sins and purify us from all unrighteousness. (1 John 1:9)

As a young teen, I had a Sunday school teacher who claimed he sometimes would go an entire day without sinning. Granted, he didn't claim to be without sin, only that he had some days where he avoided it.

Though he was a godly man and I respected him deeply, I questioned if such a thing were possible. At least I doubted it was for me. It could be I was too sensitive to sin or wrongly confused temptation with sin, but I wondered if I could even go one hour without sinning, let alone twenty-four.

Today's trio of verses addresses sin and our attitude toward it. This passage opens and closes with parallel verses that restate the same idea: if we claim to live a life without sin, we delude ourselves. (My teacher only claimed to be sinless for a day, not a lifetime.)

Scripture says that everyone has sinned and falls short of God's expectations (Romans 3:23). Therefore, if we claim we're sinless, we make God out to be a liar and do not accept his truth.

Fortunately, we don't need to wallow in our sinfulness. Sandwiched between these two verses about our sin-filled nature, we find a most encouraging promise.

John says if we confess our sins, God will forgive them, purifying us from our unrighteousness, that is, from our wrong behavior. We can count on it.

John also writes that Jesus died for the sins of the entire world (1 John 2:2), but we don't automatically receive his forgiveness. Through this sacrificial death, Jesus has prepared the gift of salvation for everyone. But until we receive his present it's not ours.

We can receive Jesus's gift of salvation when we

admit our faults. But to do that, we must first acknowledge that our sins need forgiving.

When we confess our sins, that is, admit our faults to Jesus, we can have confidence in his response of forgiveness. This is because he's already died for our sins to make us right with Father God. He will be faithful to forgive. And his forgiveness is because his death satisfied what justice demands. This is what it means when John writes that Jesus is faithful and just.

When we confess our sins, we will receive his forgiveness. This purifies us from all the wrongs we have done and all the wrong things we will do.

Have we confessed our sins to Jesus and received his forgiveness? How should we live our life knowing that he has purified us from our unrighteousness?

[Discover more about confession in Psalm 32:5, Proverbs 28:13, and Acts 19:18.]

DAY 6: OUR ADVOCATE
1 JOHN 2:1–2

But if anybody does sin, we have an advocate with the Father —Jesus Christ, the Righteous One. (1 John 2:1)

John's desire for us is that we do not sin. That's one of the reasons he writes his letter. Yet if anyone does sin, he reminds us that we have an advocate to represent us to the Father. Our advocate is none other than the righteous Jesus who sacrificed his life to atone for our sins and for the sins of the entire world.

In a general sense, an advocate is someone who represents us to a person of authority. This may be because we lack access to them or don't have the ability to properly plead our case. We need someone to stand in for us and speak on our behalf.

A lawyer is a familiar advocate in our world today, often in the courtroom. Lawyers are expensive and can't guarantee a successful outcome. However, we'll realize a much better chance of winning with a lawyer representing us than if we tried to represent ourselves. The lawyer advocates on our behalf.

In a spiritual sense, Jesus is our advocate before his Father. Imagine Jesus standing up when we sin, reminding Papa that he already atoned for them. And since we've confessed them, God remembers them no more; he wipes our slate clean.

This is a comforting thought that gives me much assurance, yet I'm not sure if it's necessary. After all, Jesus and the Father are one, so they both know what the other is thinking. Jesus doesn't need to remind his Father of anything. Father God already knows.

Yet I like the idea of Jesus as our advocate. If Jesus is for us, who can be against us? (See Romans 8:31).

Most of the time when the Bible uses the word *advocate*, however, it's not in reference to Jesus but instead to the Holy Spirit. The Holy Spirit is also our advocate. How amazing is it that we have both the Spirit and Jesus to advocate for us?

And unlike our human advocates here on earth who are expensive to hire and don't always succeed, our spiritual advocates work for us at no cost and have a much higher success rate—I suspect 100 percent.

When we sin—and we will—we need to confess it. Then we can push aside our guilt, because Jesus has already died for that sin, and the Father has forgiven it. In addition, Jesus (and the Holy Spirit) advocates on our behalf. We can't lose.

How should we react to the idea of Jesus being our advocate? When have we last thanked him for being our atoning sacrifice?

[Discover more about our advocate in Job 16:19, John 14:16, John 14:26, John 15:26, and John 16:7. Yes, most of Scripture's references to *advocate* come from John's writings.]

DAY 7: BE LIKE JESUS
1 JOHN 2:3–6

Whoever claims to live in him must live as Jesus did.
(1 John 2:6)

Today's passage talks about knowing God and keeping his commands. If we claim to know God and don't do what he says, we're only deluding ourselves from the truth, and our claim is false. But when we obey his commands our love for God is complete.

In short, as his followers, we must live as he lived. We must be like Jesus.

We are fortunate to have four biographies of Jesus in the Bible to inform us about how he lived.

They are the books of Matthew, Mark, Luke, and John. By reading them we know what Jesus does during his time here on earth. Then we can follow his example and be more like him.

We don't have to follow a bunch of rules with legalistic fervor or adhere to an extensive list of ritualistic commands like we find in the Old Testament. We must simply be like Jesus. It's that easy.

Here are some of the things that Jesus does:

- Jesus makes his relationship with his Father a priority. From an early age, Jesus puts his Father in heaven first (Luke 2:49). This is what matters most.
- Jesus takes care of himself so that he can take care of his followers. Jesus knows that if he isn't spiritually healthy, he can't expect to be at his best to help others (Matthew 14:23).
- Jesus has time for everyone who comes to him. While going to heal Jairus's daughter, he pauses to heal a sick woman (Luke 8:40–56). He stays in Samaria for two extra days simply because the people ask him to (John 4:40).

- Jesus teaches others about God. Jesus speaks with authority and not like other religious leaders (Mark 1:22). He instructs people using parables (Mark 4:2). His longest message in the Bible is the Sermon on the Mount (Matthew 5–7).
- Jesus heals others (Matthew 8:14–15). And he says his followers will do the same (John 14:12).
- Jesus opposes religious hypocrisy (Luke 13:15).
- Jesus offers love to everyone (Mark 10:21 and John 11:3–5).
- Jesus forgives and doesn't judge (John 8:3–11).
- Jesus is never in a hurry (John 11:6).
- Jesus models right behavior for his disciples and followers (John 13:15).

By following these examples of Jesus, we can live as Jesus models for us and know that we are in him.

What can we do to be more like Jesus? What must we stop doing?

[Discover more about being an example in 1 Corinthians 11:1 and 1 Peter 2:21.]

DAY 8: LOVE YOUR BROTHER AND SISTER
1 JOHN 2:7–11

Anyone who loves their brother and sister lives in the light, and there is nothing in them to make them stumble. (1 John 2:10)

John launches into a discussion about an old command and not a new one. Then he pivots just as quickly to talk about a new command. Which is it? This is confusing until we realize who the author is. John delights in tapping our imaginations with his playful, poetic prose.

As such, the old command and the new command are one in the same. But John doesn't tell us what this old/new command is. At least not in this passage. Elsewhere in his letter, it's clear that this command is love.

He says this most clearly in 1 John 3:11 when he says the old command, which we've heard from the beginning, is to love one another. Later, in 1 John 3:23, he writes that we are to believe in Jesus and love one another, just as he commanded us to live.

To discover more about the old part of this command to love, all we need to do is look at the Old Testament. In a broad sense, all the commands we read there either relate to loving God or loving others, our brothers and sisters.

Many of the Old Testament commands prescribe the right way to worship God—that is to love him properly—through their rituals and celebrations. The rest of the Old Testament commands instruct the people how to rightly interact with others—that is, to love them properly through their daily interactions.

We even find these two aspects of love when we look at the Ten Commandments. The first four commands relate to our relationship with God, which is loving *him*. The last six relate to our relationship with others, which is loving *them*.

With this as our background, Jesus arrives on earth. He personifies love to his creation. His life and teaching all relate to love, modeling it for us to follow.

When asked what Old Testament command is the most important, Jesus says to love God with all our heart, soul, mind, and strength. Then he tacks on a second one, to love our neighbors as much as we love ourselves. Everything else we read in Scripture flows from these two commands, and they stand as the greatest of all (Matthew 22:36–40 and Mark 12:28–31).

Anyone who claims to follow Jesus—that is, follows the light or walks in the light of Jesus—but doesn't love his brothers and sisters is still in darkness. Yet when we love our brothers and sisters as he commanded us, we prove that we walk in his light.

And when we live in the light, we will not stumble.

Are our lives marked by the love of Jesus? In the same way that Jesus loved us, who do we need to do a better job at loving?

[Discover more about love in John 15:13 and 1 John 3:16.]

BONUS CONTENT: I WRITE TO YOU

I am writing to you . . . (1 John 2:12–14)

A topic that keeps popping up in John's first letter is the reason he's writing. He explains it in five passages, and each time it's different.

The first reason he writes is to make his joy complete (1 John 1:4). We talked about this in Day 3.

Later he says he writes so that we will not sin (1 John 2:1). We discussed this in Day 6.

He also writes to remind us of the truth that we already know (1 John 2:21). We'll touch on this in Day 10.

And he writes so that we'll believe in Jesus and receive eternal life (1 John 5:13). We'll address this in Day 27.

The fifth passage—located between the other four—offers a trio of parallel reasons in six thoughts (1 John 2:12–14). The repetition is for emphasis. Many versions of the Bible use exclusive language in this passage, while others use inclusive labels. We'll use inclusive wording.

This triad of thoughts addresses three groups of people: children, parents (or any adult with spiritual offspring, which should be everyone), and young people. John writes for each of these.

He wants children to know they've been forgiven through Jesus because of the Father.

He wants parents to remember that they know Jesus.

And he wants young people to know that because the word of God lives in them, they are strong and have overcome the evil one.

These are some powerful reminders that we should all take hold of.

Which of these reasons for John writing do we best connect with? Which one deserves further consideration?

[Discover the reason behind some other New Testament books in Luke 1:1–4, John 20:30–31, Jude 1:3, and Revelation 1:10–11.]

DAY 9: LOVE NOT THE WORLD
1 JOHN 2:15–17

Do not love the world or anything in the world. (1 John 2:15)

John reminds his audience to not love the world or anything in it. Loving what the world offers is incompatible with loving God, as Jesus commands us to do.

We can't have the world's love and the Father's love inside us at the same time. Jesus says we cannot serve two masters, for we can only love one at a time and will therefore hate the other (Matthew 6:24 and Luke 16:13). Though Jesus talks about the love of money in these two passages, loving money exemplifies loving the things of the world.

In his prayer just before his execution, Jesus acknowledges that his disciples and followers are not of this world, just as he is not of this world (John 17:16). The same applies to us today. If we are not of this world, why should we love what it offers?

John mentions three worldly temptations we should guard against: the lust of the flesh, the lust of the eyes, and the pride of life (1 John 2:16).

The Lust of the Flesh

The lust of the flesh refers to a physical craving or desire. It's a longing to find satisfaction or fulfillment from the world that we live in. We can think of this as pursuing our old sinful nature even though we have a new nature through Jesus. We must put on our new self, one that aligns with our Lord (Colossians 3:10).

The Lust of the Eyes

Just as our body can lust, so too can our eyes. The things we look at can distract us from Jesus. We covet what we see in the world around us, craving what others have. We want to be like them and have what they have.

This can include wealth, possessions, and relationships. Though these pursuits have their place, when we chase them with wrong motives or out of a disregard for others, we live with a worldly focus that does not honor Jesus.

The Pride of Life

The third category addresses our own arrogance over what we've done, the things we own, and the esteem we receive from others. We want to impress them, to impress the world, with our accumulations and standings. The lust of the eyes feeds into the pride of life.

Though we live in the world, we need to not act as the world does or let its many sinful distractions influence us. These things are temporary, but what we do for God lives on.

That's why it's important to not love the world or anything in it.

Which of these three areas do we struggle with the most? What worldly pursuits do we need to turn away from?

[Discover more about loving the world in John 12:25, John 15:19, and 2 Timothy 4:9–10. Then read what God did out of love for his world in John 3:16–17.]

DAY 10: ANTICHRISTS
1 JOHN 2:18–23

As you have heard that the antichrist is coming, even now many antichrists have come. (1 John 2:18)

After John tells us to not love the world, he warns us about antichrists too. *Anti* means *against* and *Christ* means *Messiah*. Therefore, an antichrist is someone who is against the Messiah, that is, someone who opposes Jesus and his saving work. We can also think of the antichrist as someone who is antichristian or who opposes Jesus's church.

John affirms that there is one antichrist who is coming, as in *the* antichrist. Yet many antichrists will precede him—both then and now.

They have not come from the world, from outside our community, to oppose us. Instead, they originate from within. They were once part of Jesus's church but left, proving that they were never part of it to begin with. Who are these antichrists? Anyone who denies that Jesus is our Messiah. And by denying him they also deny the Father who sent him.

The opposite of denying Jesus is to acknowledge him. In doing so we have the Father as well. Jesus's church includes all who acknowledge him.

The word *antichrist* only shows up in four verses in the Bible, all of them written by John—two of which are in today's passage. Since John also wrote the book of Revelation, you may assume he talks about the antichrist in his end-time depiction. He does not.

Though he may allude to the antichrist, John doesn't mention him once by name in his epic prophecy about the last days. The beast in John's vision may be the antichrist (Revelation 11:7), or he may be the dragon (Revelation 13:1). Which is it?

In parallel fashion, Paul talks about "the man of lawlessness," one doomed for destruction (2 Thessalonians 2:3–4). Based on Paul's description, this person sounds much like one who is against Jesus, as in the antichrist—or at least *an* antichrist.

Further, Daniel's vision in the Old Testament describes a beast who will speak against the Lord and persecute his people (Daniel 7:23–25). Some Bible scholars view this as a prophecy about the antichrist.

Jesus, in his own end-time prophecy, warns his followers to make sure that no one deceives them by claiming to be him (Matthew 24:4–5, Mark 13:5–6, and Luke 21:8). Are these antichrists? Could one of them be *the* antichrist?

Any of these biblical passages could be what John alludes to when he says that we've already heard the antichrist is coming. Being warned, we must guard against being deceived by anyone who speaks against Jesus, whether *an* antichrist or *the* antichrist.

Sandwiched in the middle of John's teaching about the antichrist is a comforting reminder that we have the anointing from the Holy One. This is the Holy Spirit Father God sent us when Jesus returned to heaven (Luke 24:49 and John 15:26). This Holy Spirit anointing tells us what is true. We covered this in Day 6.

The opposite of this Holy Spirit truth is a lie.

Anyone who denies that Jesus is our Messiah is a liar and an antichrist.

How should we react to John's teaching about these antichrists? How can we rely on the Holy Spirit to reveal God's truth to us?

[Discover more about antichrists in the Bible's other two mentions in 1 John 4:3 and 2 John 1:7.]

DAY 11: ETERNAL LIFE
1 JOHN 2:24–25

And this is what he promised us—eternal life. (1 John 2:25)

After warning us to be on alert for the antichrist, John encourages us to make sure we hold on to the good news of Jesus—on what we heard from the beginning. We started our journey with Jesus by believing in him for the forgiveness of our sins and our salvation.

We need to hold on to this and not lose sight of it. It must remain in us. And with this good news remaining in us, we then remain in Jesus and in Papa. As a result, we will receive what Jesus promised us: eternal life.

The phrase *eternal life* doesn't occur in the Old Testament, just in the New Testament. John's biography of Jesus, the gospel of John, mentions eternal life more than any other book in the Bible. And his first letter, 1 John, comes in second. John, it seems, has much to say about eternal life. Perhaps this is because of his advancing years when we believe he wrote these two books. Or it might be that his amazing revelation from God gave him a fuller perspective of eternal life. Regardless, we should consider what John says on the subject.

Many people think of eternal life as beginning when our physical bodies die. We might do better to think of eternal life beginning as soon as we acknowledge Jesus as our Savior.

In this way we can look at three phases of eternal life.

With our life eternal beginning the day we follow Jesus, we can start our experience of eternal life today. While many Christians coast through their life, content to wait for death so they can join Jesus in heaven, they miss so much of what life with Jesus can—and should— look like now.

Our time here on earth is finite and fleeting. We must make the most of it. We do this when we tell people about Jesus, encourage others on their faith journey, and work to advance the kingdom of God. There's so much to do. Let's make every moment count.

The second aspect of eternal life begins at our death. When our time here on earth is over, we will join Jesus in his spiritual paradise. This will happen immediately for us, just like it did for the thief on the cross (Luke 23:43). This heaven exists now, and we need not wait for it to materialize at some future date. Jesus is there waiting for us to join him, just as with Stephen (Acts 7:55–56). What a glorious day that will be.

Yet this paradise is not our final home, but our temporary residence. At the end of this age, we will experience a new heaven and a new earth. This is the third and never-ending part of our eternal life.

We'll live there with Jesus and Father God (Revelation 21:3–5). In this new heaven God will wipe away our tears. We will no longer experience death, mourning, crying, or pain. Those things are gone as God makes all things new (Revelation 21:5–10).

Are we making the most of our remaining time here on earth for Jesus? What temporal pursuits should we stop doing to make room for spiritual activities that matter more?

[Discover more about eternal life in Matthew 19:29, John 3:15–17, Romans 6:22–23, and 1 Timothy 6:12. Read more about paradise in 2 Corinthians 12:3–4 and Revelation 2:7.]

DAY 12: HOLY SPIRIT ANOINTING
1 JOHN 2:26–29

The anointing you received from him remains in you, and you do not need anyone to teach you. (1 John 2:27)

Our verse for today contains two words that we've already read in 1 John 2: *anointing* and *remain*.

In verse twenty, John reminds us of the fact that we received the anointing from the Holy One, that is, the Holy Spirit (1 John 2:20). John builds on this truth in today's passage.

The other word is *remain*. John has encouraged us—implored us—to hold on to what we've heard from the beginning, to ensure it remains in us. In this way we'll remain in the Son and the Father so that we may receive the eternal life Jesus promised (1 John 2:24–25).

Now John ties these two thoughts together.

He wants to make sure that the anointing we received—the Holy Spirit—remains in us. This anointing is real and not fake. We can count on it. We need to remain in him just as we need to be certain this anointing stays with us.

The reason to remain in Holy Spirit anointing is in the middle of this passage and is easy to pass by. But don't skip it. It's important.

When the Holy Spirit's anointing remains in us, we do not need anyone to teach us. Instead of needing human instructors, the Holy Spirit will tell us all we need to know.

I repeat, through the Holy Spirit we do not need anyone to teach us. The Bible says so.

Most people who go to church do so for the music or the message. For the latter, they go so they can hear a professional member of the clergy teach them about God.

Yet John makes it clear that when we have the anointing of God's Holy Spirit, we don't need ministers to teach us. We need to teach ourselves—

to feed ourselves—not depend on someone else to do it (1 Corinthians 3:2, Hebrews 5:12–14, and 1 Peter 2:2–3).

This isn't to suggest that listening to sermons is bad. But we shouldn't depend on other people as our only source of biblical teaching. Instead, we should rely on the Holy Spirit as our principal source of spiritual truth. Teaching from others should come secondary, if needed at all.

Jesus confirms this.

He promises that Father God will send to us the Holy Spirit, who will teach us all things and help us remember what Jesus said (John 14:26). The Holy Spirit arrives at Pentecost, just as Jesus promised. And the Holy Spirit is still in our world today, teaching us what we need to know.

As we read, study, and meditate on Scripture, we should do so in tandem with the Holy Spirit. We should seek his guidance to help us understand the Bible. Some things he reveals right away, and other things unfold over time. And when we struggle to recall a passage of Scripture—especially the words of Jesus—the Holy Spirit will remind us of the text.

How well do we do on relying on the Holy Spirit to teach us? If we depend on others to instruct, while excluding the Holy Spirit, what must change?

[Discover more about God sending us the Holy Spirit in John 6:63, John 14:16–17, and John 15:26.]

BONUS CONTENT: DEAR CHILDREN

And now, dear children . . . (1 John 2:28)

In his first letter, John often uses an intimate greeting to reflect his personal affection toward his audience, toward us. Nine times he addresses us as "dear children." This term of endearment only occurs two other times throughout the rest of Scripture.

Here are the verses where John calls us "dear children."

- 1 John 2:1
- 1 John 2:12
- 1 John 2:14

- 1 John 2:18
- 1 John 2:28
- 1 John 3:7
- 1 John 3:18
- 1 John 4:4
- 1 John 5:21

John uses a similar phrase by calling us "dear friends." He does this six times. This phrase occurs in several other New Testament books, but none as often as in 1 John.

Here is where John calls us "dear friends."

- 1 John 2:7
- 1 John 3:2
- 1 John 3:21
- 1 John 4:1
- 1 John 4:7
- 1 John 4:11

John doesn't write to us from a distant vantage or with a detached perspective. Instead, he chooses to connect with us in a warm way as cherished friends, using the affectionate terms *dear children* and *dear friends*.

How should John calling us dear children *and* dear friends *inform how we receive his message? How can we adapt this perspective when we talk to other people about Jesus?*

[Discover two other times when a Bible writer calls us dear children in 1 Corinthians 4:14 and Galatians 4:19.]

DAY 13: CHILDREN OF GOD

1 JOHN 3:1–3

See what great love the Father has lavished on us, that we should be called children of God! (1 John 3:1)

The Bible says that Jesus is God's one and only Son (John 3:16–18 and 1 John 4:9). However, God also calls us his children. How can we be God's children if he has only one Son?

The Bible is full of paradoxes, but this isn't one of them.

Scripture gives us two explanations for this seeming contradiction.

The first is adoption.

In another letter, Paul writes that, through the

Holy Spirit living in us, we're adopted as children into God's family. We can call him Father, Abba, or even Papa (Romans 8:15).

Parents of biological children accept whatever God blesses them with. Parents of adopted children make a conscious decision to accept them and bring them into their family. They are children by the choice of their adoptive parents. They are chosen.

In the same way, God chooses us to be his children. He adopts us into his family.

Another truth builds on this, giving us a second way to understand how God can have only one Son yet many children. The other metaphor to aid us in our understanding of our relationship with God is that of a bride and groom, with Jesus being the groom and we, the church, being his bride.

By virtue of this holy, spiritual union, Jesus, the only Son of God, brings the church into his family through marriage. This makes us, his church, the children of God through our union with the Lamb of God, that is, the Son of God.

As such, we are indeed God's children. Scripture confirms it.

This first occurs when God adopts us into his family through the Holy Spirit. The second will occur when we, as God's church, marry his Son.

Our marriage to the Son makes us children of the Father.

We are first adopted into God's family and will later marry into it, doubly confirming us as children of God.

How can we find comfort knowing that Father God chose us and adopted us to be his sons and daughters? What are the implications that we will one day spiritually marry God's Son?

[Discover more about our adoption in Romans 8:23, Romans 9:3–4, Galatians 4:4–5, and Ephesians 1:4–6. Read about us being Jesus's bride in Revelation 19:6–8.]

DAY 14: JESUS TAKES AWAY OUR SINS
1 JOHN 3:4–5

*But you know that he appeared so that he might take away
our sins.* (1 John 3:5)

J ohn reminds us that anyone who sins breaks
the law. He's talking about the law of
Moses. Sin is something we all do. We're all
guilty of breaking God's law.

The Old Testament of the Bible—especially the
first five books—tells us in immense detail what to
do and what not to do. A failure to follow these
rules is a sin, be it a sin of commission (doing the
wrong thing) or a sin of omission (not doing the
right thing). No one can obey every one of these
Old Testament rules. This means that everyone has

sinned and falls short of meeting God's expectations (Romans 3:22–24).

To address this, God gave them an annual rite, a ceremony to symbolically take away the people's sins. This solution was temporary; it needed to be repeated each year. As such, the annual animal sacrifice gave only a partial response to take away the people's sins—to make atonement (amends) for their mistakes (Leviticus 16:34).

Each year the people sinned—every one of them—whether in big ways or small. Even the tiniest slipup made them guilty of breaking the entire law (James 2:10).

Each year, everyone fell short of what the law decreed. Each year the annual sacrifice would cleanse them from their sins for the prior twelve months. Then they'd repeat the process one year later. This continued year after year, throughout their entire lives, giving them only brief reprieves from the guilt of their sins.

This is why Jesus arrived here on our planet over two thousand years ago. Our Savior lowered himself to come to earth and walk among us, his creation. He became God in flesh and lived among us (John 1:14).

He did this to offer a permanent solution to the

problem of our sins. He died as the ultimate sin sacrifice—not an animal sacrifice, but a far pricier human one. In this way Jesus permanently took away our sins. It served as a final act, a conclusive sacrifice for our sins.

Jesus came to earth so that he could die in our place to take away our sins. His once-and-for-all sacrifice removes all our guilt, both past and present —the mistakes we have committed and the mistakes we will commit.

How should we act, knowing that Jesus took away our sins? Although Jesus freed us from our sins, in what ways do we let them continue to weigh us down?

[Discover more about the law and sacrifice for our sins in Romans 5:20–21 and Hebrews 10:1–18.]

DAY 15: DESTROYING THE WORK OF THE DEVIL

1 JOHN 3:6–10

The reason the Son of God appeared was to destroy the devil's work. (1 John 3:8)

Our passage for the day is one that troubles most people. It talks about sin. John writes that when Jesus lives in us, we won't keep on sinning. If we know him, we can't. By doing what is right, we prove we're a child of God. But if we don't do what's right, we're not his children.

Ouch! That's convicting.

Some well-intentioned teachers try to explain this verse away. They say it doesn't mean *all* sin. Instead, it refers to *habitual* sin or *intentional* sin. Yet even with these rationalizations, we may still have a reason to worry. But John doesn't give us those explanations. He says *sin*, period. Therefore, it's wrong to try to reinterpret this passage through our perspective or what we wish it said.

Paul, however, gives us some help. He says we are spirit, soul, and body (1 Thessalonians 5:23). That is, we are a spirit, we have a soul, and we live in a body.

When we repent of our wrongdoing (our sin) to follow Jesus, our spirit is immediately and permanently made sinless. The spirit part of us is sanctified—that is, made right and set apart as holy—as soon as we believe in Jesus as our Savior. Theologians call this *positional* sanctification.

Yet this doesn't address our soul and our body.

Our soul—comprising our mind, will, and emotions—begins to align with our sanctified spirit. This is a process of *ongoing* sanctification.

Our body is the last to move toward the sinless condition of our spirit. This is a lifetime process, but through God's grace we can inch closer to it each day.

Tucked in the middle of this passage, however, is the key to this issue of sin. John reminds us that

Jesus—the Son of God—came to destroy the work of the devil. Jesus came to overcome sin.

He sets this in motion when he dies on the cross as the ultimate sin sacrifice. As a result, he takes away our sins—past, present, and future—to make us right with Father God. This is the first phase of destroying the devil's work. Yet it won't become final until we reach the end of time when Satan is tossed into the lake of burning sulfur (Revelation 20:10) so that God can usher in a new heaven and a new earth (Revelation 21:1).

The work of Jesus to defeat Satan began two thousand years ago, yet it remains in process today. So too is our sanctification, our moving from a sinful life to a sinless future. God will complete this for us, just as he will one day conclusively deal with the devil.

God will sanctify us through and through (1 Thessalonians 5:23).

John later writes that when we acknowledge Jesus as God's Son, he lives in us and we in him (1 John 4:15). John doesn't mention sin in this verse. This is because through the sanctifying work of the Holy Spirit, sin no longer needs to be an issue for us.

What is our view of sin and how should we let God's Word inform our perspective? What are we doing to allow the sanctifying work of the Holy Spirit to move us toward sinlessness?

[Discover more about sanctification in John 17:17–19, Romans 15:16, 1 Corinthians 6:11, and 1 Peter 1:1–2.]

DAY 16: LOVE ONE ANOTHER
1 JOHN 3:11–15

For this is the message you heard from the beginning: We should love one another. (1 John 3:11)

J ohn tells his audience that we are to love one another.

It's not a new command but one we've heard from the beginning. He first mentions this in 1 John 2:7–8. And now he tells us what this command is: we are to love one another. It's that simple.

Saying that we've heard this from "the beginning" centers on Jesus.

When an expert in the law asks Jesus to name the greatest command, he says it's to love God.

Then he tacks on a second one—which makes it the second greatest command—to love others. In a most effective manner, these summarize everything in the Old Testament (Matthew 22:35–40).

We are to love God and love one another.

Jesus also talks about the importance of loving one another in his Sermon on the Mount. In that message he tells his listeners to love others in the same way that they love themselves (Matthew 7:12). He says the same thing, although more succinctly, in his Sermon on the Plain (Luke 6:31).

Though it's through Jesus that we get this essential command to love one another, we find it throughout the Old Testament. All the commands God gives his people either relate to their relationship with him or their relationship with others. As we've already mentioned, this comes from the Ten Commandments too. We first love God (commandments one through four) and then we love others (commandments five through ten).

This is why Jesus says the greatest command is to love God and the second greatest is to love others. Everything else in the Old Testament underscores these two (Matthew 22:37–40).

We find this command to love others hidden in the Levitical law too. Quoting the words of Father

God, Moses writes that we are to love our neighbors in the same way we love ourselves (Leviticus 19:18), which Jesus later quotes in Matthew 22:39.

Paul reiterates this in his letter to the church in Rome. He says we should owe no outstanding debt other than the continuing debt to love one another. When we do this, we fulfill the Old Testament commands (Romans 13:8).

In his letter to the church in Galatia, Paul confirms that we can keep the entire law by obeying the singular command to love our neighbor as much as we love ourselves (Galatians 5:14).

This command to love one another as we love ourselves is the essence of the Golden Rule. We are to treat others the way we want them to treat us. This means doing for them the same things that we'd like to receive ourselves. It also means not doing to them the things we don't want to receive. The Golden Rule is based on the Bible, going back to Leviticus 19:18.

This idea of loving one another as we love ourselves permeates Scripture. It's been there since the beginning.

What must we do differently to more fully obey God's essential command to love our neighbor? Beyond that, how well do we obey God's greatest command to love him?

[See John's instructions to love one another in John 13:34, John 13:35, 1 John 3:11, 1 John 3:23, 1 John 4:7, 1 John 4:11, 1 John 4:12, and 2 John 1:5.]

DAY 17: WHAT LOVE IS
1 JOHN 3:16–20

This is how we know what love is: Jesus Christ laid down his life for us. And we ought to lay down our lives for our brothers and sisters. (1 John 3:16)

The ultimate expression of love is to die for another, to sacrifice ourselves for the good of someone else. Jesus exemplifies this highest form of love by dying as a human sacrifice for us—for all people, for all time. His death covers the penalty our sins deserve, thereby making us right with Father God.

In the same way, we should be willing to lay down our lives for our brothers and sisters in Christ. Yes, this may mean to actually die for them so they can live. But in practical terms our call to sacrifice may be less demanding.

John writes that we prove God's love in us when we have pity on our brother and sister in need. The most direct application is to share what we have with them, to give our possessions to those in Jesus's church—our brothers and sisters.

Having pity on them, however, doesn't always mean giving them our belongings. At times we may need to say no.

This isn't a justification to not help them with tangible solutions, but to note that giving them what they lack isn't always the answer. Sometimes our generosity could enable them to continue to make the same ill-advised decisions or persist in the same wrong behaviors that caused the situation in the first place. In these instances, the wise thing is to say no. We offer them tough love. This is how we can best take pity on them.

Another way to take pity on our brothers and sisters in need is to pray for them. As strange as it seems to say, in this case we must ensure that prayer isn't our default position but a secondary one. We get this understanding when John implores us to not love with words only but with actions and in truth (1 John 3:18). In this way we can have a clear conscience, knowing that we responded rightly and can therefore rest in God's presence.

We must remember that we are not to accumulate wealth for ourselves. Instead, we are to store up our treasures in heaven (Matthew 6:19–21). God blesses us—just as he did Father Abraham—so that we can bless others (Genesis 12:2). Yet we need to balance this with a call to be a wise steward of what God has given us (Matthew 25:14–30).

These passages give us much to contemplate when we consider how to best take pity on our brothers and sisters in need.

How can we lay down our lives for our brothers and sisters? When have we tried to help someone with our words when we should have acted?

[Discover more about Jesus's great love in laying down his life for us in John 10:11–18.]

DAY 18: JESUS'S TWO COMMANDS
1 JOHN 3:21–24

And this is his command: to believe in the name of his Son, Jesus Christ, and to love one another as he commanded us.
(1 John 3:23)

J ohn teaches us that if we have a clear conscience before God, we can be confident that we'll receive from him whatever we ask (1 John 3:21–22). We'll cover this more in Day 27, but for now, we'll look at John's reason why God will answer our prayers. It's because we keep his commands.

But this doesn't refer to the Old Testament law and the many directives we find there. Instead, it refers to a pair of commands. That's right. Just two commands rise above all others. These are what God expects us to follow. We've touched on them in our prior readings.

What are they?

The first is to believe in Jesus. The second is to love one another. When we keep these two commands, we live in him, and he lives in us.

In considering this first command—to believe in God's son, Jesus Christ—let's not make the mistake of thinking that Jesus is his first name and Christ is his second. Though *Jesus Christ* may roll off our tongues as if it's his full name, this is not the case. Christ is a descriptor of Jesus, not his name—even though we've made it into one.

Christ means Messiah (John 1:41), as in Jesus the Messiah (Mark 1:1) or Jesus *the* Christ (1 John 2:22). Therefore, when we read the instruction to believe in Jesus Christ, it means to believe in Jesus the Messiah, the Savior—essentially to believe in Jesus as *our* Messiah, *our* Savior.

The second command of John—to love one another—stands as a recurring theme of his. He's already covered it and will continue to do so. We see it throughout the book of 1 John. We've also covered this in Day 16 and touched on it in many other days.

God's two commands—to believe in Jesus as the Christ and to love one another—are consistent with Jesus's teaching about the two greatest commandments in Scripture (Matthew 22:36–40).

In a broad sense, believing in Jesus is the key way we love God, which Jesus says is the greatest Old Testament commandment. The second is to love our neighbor as ourselves. That is, we should love one another.

Have we taken the essential step to believe in Jesus as our Savior? How well do we do at obeying God's second command to love one another?

[Discover more about loving one another in 2 Thessalonians 1:3. Contrast this with Titus 3:3.]

BONUS CONTENT: THE "ONE ANOTHER" COMMANDS

Love one another as he commanded us. (1 John 3:23)

The Bible gives us over two dozen commands of how to treat one another.

The command to "love one another" occurs most often—a total of ten times, eight from the pen of John (see Day 16), with the other two from Paul and Peter (Romans 13:8 and 1 Peter 1:22).

In addition to loving one another, here are some of the other commands about how we are to treat one another:

- Accept one another (Romans 15:7).

- Instruct one another (Romans 15:14).
- Submit to one another (Ephesians 5:21).
- Forgive one another (Colossians 3:13).
- Teach one another (Jeremiah 9:20).
- Teach and admonish one another (Colossians 3:16).
- Encourage one another (Judges 20:22, 1 Thessalonians 5:11, Hebrews 3:13, and Hebrews 10:25).
- Agree with one another (1 Corinthians 1:10).
- Fellowship with one another (1 John 1:7).
- Give to one another (Esther 9:22).
- Live in harmony with one another (Romans 12:16).
- Be kind and compassionate to one another (Ephesians 4:32)
- Serve one another in love (Galatians 5:13).
- Bear with one another in love (Ephesians 4:2).
- Be devoted to one another in love (Romans 12:10).
- Honor one another above yourselves (Romans 12:10).

- Greet one another with a kiss of love (1 Peter 5:14).
- Greet one another with a holy kiss (Romans 16:16, 1 Corinthians 16:20, and 2 Corinthians 13:12).
- Speak to one another with psalms, hymns, and spiritual songs (Ephesians 5:19).
- Spur one another on toward love and good deeds (Hebrews 10:24).
- Offer hospitality to one another without grumbling (1 Peter 4:9).
- Administer justice and show mercy and compassion to one another (Zechariah 7:9).
- Wash one another's feet (John 13:14).
- Clothe yourselves with humility toward one another (1 Peter 5:5).

Given the context of these "one another" commands, we clearly see them applying to our brothers and sisters within the church of Jesus. Yet, when appropriate, we can extend these principles to embrace those outside our faith community. In this way, we can show them the love of Jesus and be a witness to them about our Savior.

Which of these "one another" commands do we need to give more attention to? What will be the results as we obey these commands?

[Discover more about our relationship with one another in Philippians 2:5–7.]

DAY 19: SPIRIT OF GOD
1 JOHN 4:1–3

This is how you can recognize the Spirit of God: Every spirit that acknowledges that Jesus Christ has come in the flesh is from God. (1 John 4:2)

The third chapter of 1 John wraps up with a reference to the Holy Spirit, whom God sent to us. John now contrasts the Holy Spirit to other spirits. These manifest in the form of false prophets—that is, purveyors of wayward doctrine. These false messages come from demons in the spiritual realm.

The Holy Spirit speaks truth to us. These contrary spirits fill us with lies. They distort who

God is and what the Bible says. Many unsuspecting believers fall victim to their twisting of the truth.

This first happened back in Genesis when the serpent (the devil) lies to Eve and misrepresents what God said to her. She foolishly believes him, and Adam passively follows her (Genesis 3:1–7). Because of Adam and Eve's failings, resulting from the serpent's mischaracterization of God's truth, sin enters our world and God expels Adam and Eve from their idyllic paradise.

John recommends that we test every spirit, that is, to test every prophet and their message. This is because many false prophets have gone out *into* the world. This implies that they started as part of Jesus's church.

John gives us a simple test. He says that every spirit—that is, every teacher—who acknowledges Jesus as the Messiah who physically came to earth in human form is from God. If someone does not recognize this truth, they are not from God. In fact, they are the antichrist—that is, anti-Christ, which is to say they are against Jesus the Messiah.

These false prophets were in the world two thousand years ago, and they're still with us today. We must be equally discerning of their error.

In addition to John's basic test to identify these

false prophets, we can also consult the Bible. In the book of Acts, Luke applauds the cautious approach of the believers in Berea in discerning between truth and error. They eagerly received Paul's message about the good news of Jesus. But because of their noble character, they examined the Scriptures (the Old Testament) to verify that what Paul claimed was correct (Acts 17:10–15).

We should follow their example to avoid the teachings of any false prophets who threaten to lead us astray.

In what ways must we be more discerning about who we listen to? What doctrines have we accepted that we need to test against what the Bible says?

[Discover more about false prophets in Matthew 7:15, Luke 6:26, Acts 13:6–12, and 2 Peter 2:1.]

DAY 20: THE GREATER POWER
1 JOHN 4:4–6

The one who is in you is greater than the one who is in the world. (1 John 4:4)

After talking about the Holy Spirit and false prophets—that is, false teachers under Satan's control—John gives us a comforting truth. As Father God's children who believe in Jesus, we have the Holy Spirit (whom John calls the Spirit of truth) living in us. Greater, John says, is the one who lives in us than the one who is in the world.

Many people don't realize this, and their behavior belies John's teaching. They view God and Satan as equal and opposing forces. They're left quaking, wondering which force will win—and praying that they haven't misplaced their faith.

Yet this perspective is incorrect. God and Satan are not equal. God, as Creator, made all the angels —including Satan, a fallen angel. The Creator is clearly superior to his creation. That's why John can confidently teach us that God—who lives in us—is more powerful than the devil who lives in the world around us.

Yes, God has granted Satan a bit of authority in our world for a time. But our Lord will one day take back that authority and punish the evil one forever.

This victory over Satan began when Jesus died in our place for the wrong things we have done, defeating death and our enemy who specializes in death (John 10:10). We'll find the finale of Jesus's victory revealed in full at the end of time, when Father God ushers in a new heaven and a new earth where we'll live forever (Revelation 21:1–2).

We must focus on God's power and Jesus's victory. John reminds us that we are children of God. As his children, our heritage comes through him. He has overcome evil, and as his children we can overcome evil too.

God is greater than the devil. The battle has already happened, and God has won. We are on the winning side. And God is in us. Through him we can overcome the evil one's opposition *and* the evil that is in the world.

We can count on God as the ultimate power and should live confident lives as a result.

In what ways do our lives show we believe we're on the winning side? When have we placed too much emphasis on the power of our enemy?

[Discover what else John says about the Spirit of truth (Holy Spirit) in John 14:16–17, John 15:26, and John 16:13.]

DAY 21: THE LOVE OF GOD
1 JOHN 4:7–12

This is how God showed his love among us: He sent his one and only Son into the world that we might live through him.
(1 John 4:9)

S o far in John's letter he's already talked a lot about love, building up to this passage in chapter four, where the topic of love becomes the focus. In the rest of chapter 4, John mentions love twenty-seven times. That's a lot of love.

Building on his encouragement to love one another from the prior chapter, John again reminds us—his dear friends—to love one another. This is because love comes from God, and he empowers us to love others. When we are born of God and know him, we're able to love others well. But those who don't know God aren't able to love.

Loving others is the fruit of our relationship with our Heavenly Father; it's proof of our right standing with him, through Jesus.

Though we love God, he loved us first (1 John 4:19). He proved this by sending his precious Son to earth so that we might live eternally through him. Father God sent Jesus into our world as the sacrifice to atone for our sins (1 John 4:10).

We often think of Jesus's great love for us. He showed this ultimate expression of love through his willingness to die in our place for all the wrong things we've done in our life—and all the wrong that we will do.

Jesus endured a most painful death, tortured at the hands of his Roman executioners. Dying in our place is the epitome of love, and we celebrate him for making this supreme sacrifice. In turn, we love him back to the best of our ability.

Yet John isn't talking about Jesus's love for us by dying in our place. Instead, the apostle is talking about Father God's great love for us. God showed his immense love for us by sending Jesus to save us.

For those of us who are parents, we don't want

to see our children suffer. We'd gladly stand in their place if we could shelter them from the pain of their struggles. Our Heavenly Father is no different from us in this regard. How hard it must have been for Father God to send his precious Son into our world, knowing what he would have to endure.

That's real love. And God's immense love for us is why we should love one another. When we do, "God lives in us and his love is made complete in us" (1 John 4:12).

How well do we do at accepting God's love for us? How well do we do at loving others?

[Discover more about God's love for us in Romans 5:7–10.]

.

DAY 22: ACKNOWLEDGE JESUS
1 JOHN 4:13–15

If anyone acknowledges that Jesus is the Son of God, God lives in them and they in God. (1 John 4:15)

In yesterday's reading John said that anyone who loves has been born of God and knows him (1 John 4:7). Later we'll read that anyone who believes in Jesus as the Messiah is born of God (1 John 5:1). And today we read that anyone who acknowledges Jesus as God's Son has God living in them (1 John 4:15).

Are these three ways to approach God in conflict? Or are they alternative options to achieve the same outcome? Neither. Instead let's view them as complementary, working in cooperation to bring about our right standing with God and our future with him in heaven.

It starts with believing in Jesus as the Messiah, as *our* Savior. We then acknowledge him as the Son of God and give testimony to others about him. The outcome of our belief and our testimony is loving others. Loving others isn't a requirement to earn our salvation. It's the result of our salvation— a natural byproduct of our faith.

The word *acknowledge* appears four times in the book of first John. This is more than any other New Testament book. (As you might expect, *acknowledge* also shows up in the gospel of John, 2 John, and Revelation, three of John's other writings.)

First, we read that whoever acknowledges Jesus as the Son of God also has the Father (1 John 2:23). It's as if they're a package. Acknowledging one acknowledges the other. Through our acknowledgment we have the Son and the Father.

Next, in 1 John 4:2–3 the word *acknowledge* comes up twice. (See our discussion about the false prophets in Day 19.) Every spirit who acknowledges Jesus as the Messiah who walked among us in human form is from God. Whereas every spirit who does not acknowledge Jesus is not from God.

Acknowledging Jesus is key.

This means our faith can't be silent. We need to tell others about the confidence we have in Jesus and what he's done for us.

At a basic level acknowledging him means to give our assent. If someone asks if we're a Christian —a believer or a follower of Jesus—we acknowledge our standing with him by saying yes. And we do so with confidence.

On a more consequential level, acknowledging means taking the initiative to tell others about Jesus. We testify about him. We are his witnesses to the world. If we don't tell them, who will?

This is what it means to acknowledge Jesus as the Son of God.

When have we been silent about Jesus when we should have spoken? How can we do a better job at acknowledging him before a world who needs him?

[Discover what John says about acknowledgment in John 9:22, John 12:42, 2 John 1:7, and Revelation 3:5 and 9.]

DAY 23: NO REASON TO FEAR
1 JOHN 4:16–18

There is no fear in love. But perfect love drives out fear.
(1 John 4:18)

In the Old Testament of the Bible, we read the command to "fear God" (Ecclesiastes 12:13). In the New Testament we see the principle to "love God" (1 Corinthians 8:3), and we read that God is love (1 John 4:8 and 16).

How can we fear someone we're supposed to love, someone who loves us? Is it even possible?

Is there a difference between fearing God in the Old Testament and loving God in the New Testament? Although it's the same God in both, one who doesn't change, the difference is Jesus. Jesus alters the way we understand and perceive God.

True, we are to fear God, and we are to love God. This is a spiritual paradox.

In the Old Testament, the focus is on the law (rules) and the result is fear because we fall short of God's expectations. Based on our failure to follow every part of the law, we deserve to die; stumbling over one small point makes us guilty of all (James 2:10). The penalty for our sins is death; it doesn't matter if it is one sin or many. This is something to fear. Under the law we can't make ourselves right to stand before God. This conclusion is the purpose of the law. It shows us our sin and the need for Jesus to save us (Romans 7:7).

In the New Testament, Jesus fulfills the law—overcomes or replaces its rules—with love. This is the immense love of Father God in sending Jesus to earth to save us and our Savior's incomprehensible love to die in our place.

The result is that love trumps fear. This doesn't mean we should disregard a healthy fear of God, but instead we should temper our fear with his love.

His love serves to push away our fear of punishment. This is because his perfect love drives out our fear.

Therefore, by faith we can have confidence on judgment day because of his love. Whoever lives a life of love has God living in them.

But we need not feel guilty if a touch of fear remains. This simply means that his love has not yet fully matured in us. But through him we move closer toward realizing his perfect love. When his love becomes complete in us, it will drive away our fear of the future and judgment.

How can God's love in us move toward completion and become perfect? What should be our attitude toward any fear that remains in us?

[Discover more about fear in Luke 1:50, Luke 12:5, Luke 23:40, Philippians 2:12, and Revelation 14:7.]

DAY 24: HE FIRST LOVED US
1 JOHN 4:19–21

We love because he first loved us. (1 John 4:19)

Perhaps the most misused, most misunderstood word in English is *love*. I love my wife, and I love to watch movies. I love nature, and I love blue. I love to write, and I love spring.

I also love God.

If our love of God means anything, we show it by how we love. This is because he loved us first. Therefore, we respond to his love by loving him back and by loving others.

We show our love to him by how we worship him, how we spend our time, and how we use the resources he blesses us with. Our love for him is a fitting response to his love for us.

We also show our love to God by obeying his commands. One of his chief instructions is for us to love one another (Day 16).

If we do not love the brothers and sisters we live with and can see, how can we expect to love the God we don't live with and can't see? We delude ourselves if we claim to love God yet remain mired in hate toward others. Therefore, if we love God, we must also love our brothers and our sisters.

We may wonder who qualifies as our brothers and sisters. Surely, this goes beyond our own family, but does it expand to include only those in our faith community, or does it mean everyone in the entire world?

We can ask the same question about the command to love one another. Does this only apply to the Church of Jesus, or does it apply to everyone?

For the answer to this question, recall the parable of the good Samaritan (Luke 10:25–37). A religious expert asks Jesus what he must do to inherit eternal life. Jesus tells him to love God fully and to love his neighbor as much as he loves himself. The religious expert asks Jesus to define *neighbor*. This is when Jesus gives his parable.

It's a story about a man who's robbed and left on the side of the road to die. A priest comes upon the man but walks by him. Next a Levite arrives and ignores the hurting man as well. At last, a Samaritan—a person Jesus's audience reviled—arrives on the scene. He stops to help the man and takes steps to nurse him back to health.

Jesus asks the religious expert which of these three people acted as a good neighbor to the injured man.

The religious leader can't bear to even say "the Samaritan man." Instead, he simply says, "The one who showed mercy."

Jesus tells him to do likewise.

In the same way we should love one another—our brothers and sisters—because God first loved us.

In what ways do we misuse the word love? *How can we love God more fully and our brothers and sisters better?*

[Discover more about loving our neighbors in Galatians 5:14.]

DAY 25: OVERCOME THE WORLD
1 JOHN 5:1–5

Everyone born of God overcomes the world. (1 John 5:4)

There is a lot packed into today's passage, but most of it reviews what John has already written. He talks about believing in Jesus as our Savior (the Christ) for us to be born again. How loving the Father is loving his Son. There's a reminder to love others and obey God's commands, which are easy to do and not a burden (see Day 18).

Then John slides in the word *overcome*. He's already mentioned this word in two passages.

First, he said that the word of God lives in us, and we have overcome the evil one (1 John 2:13–

14). Second, he said that since we are from God—that is, his children—we have overcome the spirit of false prophets, the antichrists (1 John 4:1–4).

For his third mention of *overcome*, John does not build on either of these prior mentions. Instead, he adds a third consideration, one even more grand. He says that everyone born of God overcomes the world. Yes, we, through our belief in Jesus as God's Son, have overcome the world. Not that we *can*, not that we *might*, but that we *are* actually doing so. We are overcoming the world.

From a spiritual sense we will overcome the world as we move closer to our time of joining Jesus in heaven. From a tangible perspective we overcome the world each day—at least that's God's expectation.

Yet many Christians don't act as though they're overcoming the world. Instead, they live defeated, dejected lives that prove how the world has overcome them. I get that. I've been there. But that's not God's plan; this is not his intent.

Everyone born of God overcomes the world. Not a few. Not some. Not even most. Everyone. Everyone who believes that Jesus is the Son of God has this overcome-the-world condition in them.

Then why don't our lives show it? Or show it more often?

I wonder if it's because we try to live a life that's too close to the world we hope to overcome. If we act like the world and think like the world, it's impossible to overcome the world because we are part of it; we're fully immersed in it.

But this isn't a call to segregate ourselves from our worldly neighbors, community, and society. If we do that, we'll never have a chance to tell them about Jesus. Yes, we must stay in our world, but if we're too much like it, our witness will be ineffective, and we'll have no hope of overcoming the world.

Are we overcoming the world or is it overcoming us? What should we do to be less like the world and more likely to be a witness for Jesus to the world?

[Discover what else John writes about *overcome* in John 1:5 and John 16:33.]

DAY 26: THREE WITNESSES GIVE TESTIMONY

1 JOHN 5:6–12

For there are three that testify: the Spirit, the water and the blood; and the three are in agreement. (1 John 5:7–8)

The Old Testament gives a rule that to convict someone requires two or three witnesses (Deuteronomy 19:15). The testimony of one person is not enough. Two people must agree; three are better. This principle of multiple witnesses repeats throughout the Bible.

John builds on this standard of three witnesses by telling us of those who testify about Jesus. These are not human witnesses but supernatural ones. In this case, the trio testifying of Jesus is comprised of the Spirit, the water, and the blood.

The first witness is the Spirit, as in the Holy Spirit, the Spirit of truth. The Old Testament testifies often about Jesus, but most people in Jesus's day miss it (John 5:39–40). It takes the work of the Holy Spirit for them to understand what Scripture says about Jesus. The same is true today. The Holy Spirit serves as Jesus's first witness.

The second to give testimony is the water. This references Jesus's baptism. Many were baptized around the time of Jesus and many more have been baptized since. What makes Jesus's baptism special? First, sinless Jesus doesn't need to repent for his sins, which is the purpose of John's baptism. More important is that after John baptizes Jesus, Father God speaks from heaven. He testifies about Jesus, as his Son whom he loves and is most pleased with (Matthew 3:16–17, Mark 1:10–11, and Luke 3:21–22). The Father, speaking at Jesus's baptism, serves as the second witness.

The third to give testimony is the blood. This references Jesus's death. Though not common, it's possible one person—any person—could choose to die in place of another. Yet this sacrifice would be incomplete, just like the annual sin sacrifices prescribed in the Old Testament. What makes Jesus's sacrificial death different? What makes his death the ultimate sacrifice to end all sacrifices? Quite simply, Jesus doesn't just die. He overcomes death by rising from the dead. His resurrection shows his mastery over death, both his and ours (Romans 6:9). This serves as the third witness.

These three witnesses—Spirit, water, and blood—agree in their testimony of Jesus.

If we're willing to believe in the witness of three people, we should put even more confidence in the testimony of three supernatural witnesses.

Jesus died so that we may live.

How willing are we to believe what God says over what people say? Which of the three witnesses for Jesus do we best connect with? Why?

[Discover what else John writes about witnesses for Jesus in John 8:18.]

BONUS CONTENT: WHOEVER HAS THE SON HAS LIFE

Whoever has the Son has life; whoever does not have the Son of God does not have life. (1 John 5:12)

In the first of John's three letters, he writes to the early followers of Jesus, reminding them of God's essential message about Jesus, light, and life. Jesus is the light, and he gives life. So, amid John's poetic prowess, his words all revolve around Jesus—the Son who gives life.

As John winds down his letter, he writes that whoever has the Son has life, but whoever doesn't have Jesus doesn't. John says the same thing in his biography of Jesus (John 3:36).

We take this word *life* to mean eternal life, that is, our future reality in heaven.

Yes, it is that. But this future begins today, not after we die.

The life Jesus gives us is physical life too. And this might be just as important.

Too many Christians plod through this life, placing all their hopes on their future existence in heaven. But their exclusive future focus robs them of what God wants to give them today.

We need to make the most of this life Jesus gives us:

- Live for him.
- Love others as he loves us.
- Point them to Jesus.

John states it so simply, and Jesus makes it so easy: Whoever has the Son has life.

Do you have the Son? If so, the life he gives starts here, now. If not, seek Jesus and you will have life. It's that simple.

[Discover more about having life through Jesus in John 3:16–17, John 6:40, and John 20:30–31.]

DAY 27: ASK ANYTHING
ACCORDING TO GOD'S WILL
1 JOHN 5:13–15

If we ask anything according to his will, he hears us. (1 John 5:14)

When we pray, do we think God hears us? Does he answer our prayers? All of them? The Bible says so. Consider what Scripture teaches.

First, we can have assurance that God does indeed hear our prayers.

John writes that we can be confident God will hear everything we ask and will grant everything we request. But there's a condition that's easy to miss, and it's a critical one. John stipulates that God will hear our prayers and answer them when we align our requests with his will (1 John 5:14–15).

The challenge for us then is to discover his perspective and pray according to his will. This may not be as hard as we think. Paul writes that we already have the mind of Christ through the Holy Spirit (1 Corinthians 2:14–16).

The Holy Spirit can reveal to us the will of God. It's simple. Each thing the Holy Spirit tells us to do is the will of God. We can count on this because God would never tell us to do something contrary to his will. For some followers of Jesus, hearing the Holy Spirit is a daily part of life, while others struggle to hear from God, even once. But we should all lean into this and be open to hear from the Holy Spirit. In this way we will know the will of God.

Another way to know the will of God is to read his written word, the Bible. The Father also reveals his will to us through Scripture. For example, he is not willing that anyone should perish (Matthew 18:14). Therefore, it's aligned with his will to pray for the salvation of others. But we must also act according to our prayers. We plant (tell them about Jesus) and then trust God to make the crop grow

(1 Corinthians 3:6) and produce a harvest (2 Corinthians 9:10).

A third way to know the will of God is to spend time with him. As we do, we will get to know him better and develop a stronger sense for what he wants, for his perspective, and for his will. Enoch can serve as our example in this. He walked so close to God that the Almighty whisked his faithful follower into heaven (Genesis 5:22–24).

We find a fourth way to know God's will—his good, pleasing, and perfect will—is to not conform to the world, but to transform our thinking by renewing our minds. When we do this, we'll understand what God's will is (Romans 12:2).

In these four ways we can know God's will.

When our prayers align with his will, he will answer our requests. But answered prayer isn't the goal; it's the outcome. Our aim should be to know God's will. May we focus on that.

How do we react when God doesn't answer our prayers the way we want and when we want? What should we do to better align our perspective with the will of God?

[Discover more about God answering our prayers in 1 John 3:21–22.]

DAY 28: THE SIN THAT LEADS TO DEATH

1 JOHN 5:16–17

There is a sin that leads to death. (1 John 5:16)

Today's passage teaches us some unusual things about prayer.

First, John encourages us to pray for others when we notice sin in their lives. This isn't all people, but our brothers and sisters in Jesus. Then God will give them life. I don't think I've ever prayed for others in this way. Even so, I've heard the plaintive prayers of parents over the sins of a wayward child.

Yet this praying for the sins of others isn't just John's idea. James gives a similar instruction. He tells us to confess our sins to each other and pray for one another. Then we'll receive healing (James 5:16). I've joined in with these kinds of prayers, but it's always because the person I'm praying for has requested it.

John and James want us to pray for the sins of other believers. Therefore, we should.

Yet these prayers are for sins that don't lead to death. John suggests that we don't pray for the sins of others that *do* lead to death.

What is a sin that leads to death? The question is enough to give us pause.

The Bible has accounts of sin that lead to immediate death. There are Ananias and Sapphira, whom God strikes down for lying to the Holy Spirit (Acts 5:1–10). There is also Herod, whom the Lord strikes down for accepting glory for himself and not giving it to God (Acts 12:21–23). A third example of immediate death occurs when Korah stirs up dissidents to oppose the leadership of Moses. God is not pleased and punishes some of them by opening the ground to swallow them. Then he sends fire from heaven to consume the rest (Numbers 16:1–35).

This sin that leads to death could also relate to the unpardonable sin that Jesus talks about: blasphemy against the Holy Spirit. The context is the religious teachers who claim Jesus drives out demons because Beelzebul, the prince of demons, possesses him. They say this instead of giving the credit to Jesus—or implicitly the Holy Spirit (Matthew 12:24–32, Mark 3:22–30, and Luke 12:10).

The unpardonable sin is blasphemy against the Holy Spirit. It dismisses or even denies Holy Spirit power and his work to produce signs and wonders. It worries me when I hear people claim that the evidentiary works of the Holy Spirit ended with the age of the apostles and no longer exist in our world today. In essence they dismiss the Holy Spirit. Are they in danger of blasphemy against him and committing the unpardonable sin?

On an imperative level, the sin that leads to death is the sin of rejecting Jesus as the Son of God and as our Messiah. Yet, as we discussed in yesterday's reading, it's God's will that none should perish, so we should pray for their salvation. Keep in mind, though, that once a person who has spurned Jesus is dead, their decision is final, and our prayers cannot overcome their permanent rejection of the Messiah. Their choice has led to their eternal death.

These ideas of sins that lead to death are all

speculation, for we can't know for sure, but we should exercise care to guard against each one.

How can we best pray for the sins of other Christians? What should be our proper perspective of Holy Spirit power?

[Discover more about sin and death in Romans 6:23, Romans 8:1–2, and Romans 8:10.]

BONUS CONTENT: THE ISSUE OF SIN

All wrongdoing is sin. (1 John 5:17)

John writes a lot about sin. He mentions it in sixteen verses in 1 John (as well as in twenty-two verses in his gospel of John).

Here are the passages where 1 John addresses sin:

- 1 John 1:7–10
- 1 John 2:1–2
- 1 John 2:12
- 1 John 3:4–9
- 1 John 4:10–11
- 1 John 5:16–18

Aligned with John's mentions of sin, we talked about it in:

- Day 4: God Is Light
- Day 5: Confess Our Sins
- Day 6: Our Advocate
- Day 14: Jesus Takes Away Our Sins
- Day 15: Destroying the Work of the Devil
- Day 28: The Sin That Leads to Death

We also mention *sin* in:

- Day 8: Bonus Content: I Write to You
- Day 19: Spirit of God
- Day 23: No Reason to Fear
- Day 26: Three Witnesses Give Testimony
- Day 29: The True God

Reading all that John writes about sin can put us on an emotional rollercoaster, vacillating between assurance and fear when it comes to sin and our relationship to it.

We covered one way to provide a balanced understanding of sin in Day 15 when we talked about sanctification in relation to our spirit, soul, and body.

If we are born of God, how should we view sin? How can we better align our thinking about sin with John's teaching on the subject?

[Discover more about what John says about sin in John 8:24 and John 8:34.]

DAY 29: THE TRUE GOD

1 JOHN 5:18–20

He is the true God and eternal life. (1 John 5:20)

Today's trio of verses each begins with the same phrasing: *We know that.*

What follows them are seven concepts John wants to remind his audience about. He has covered them throughout his letter and reinforces these key points now.

Here are John's seven statements for us to remember:

1. We know that anyone born of God does not continue to sin (verse 18). John covers the issue of sin in depth, mentioning it in twenty verses. See our recap about sin in Day 28: Bonus Content.

2. We know that those born of God will stay safe (verse 18). John uses the phrase *born of God* six times and is the only biblical writer to do so. This is analogous to being born again, which is having eternal life—another phrase John often uses. See Day 11.

3. We know that the evil one cannot harm us (verse 18). John mentions *the evil one* five times and assures us we will overcome him (1 John 2:13–14). See Day 8: Bonus Content.

4. We know that we're children of God (verse 19). John uses the endearing phrase *children of God* five times. See Day 13.

5. We know that the entire world is under the control of the evil one (verse 19). John mentions *world* in sixteen verses in this letter. He also says that God is greater than the world (1 John 4:4), so we have nothing to fear. See Day 25.

6. We know that the Son of God has come (verse 20). The focus of John's letter is on Jesus— the Son of God—coming to earth to save us, such as in 1 John 5:5–6. See Day 26: Bonus Content.

7. We know that the Son of God has given us understanding to know (verse 20). The word *know* shows up in thirty-two verses in John's letter. See Day 8: Bonus Content and Day 27.

And what is it that Jesus (and John) wants us to know?

Quite simply, they want us to know the One who is true: Jesus's Father—and our heavenly Father. We are part of him because we are part of his Son.

He is the one true God and gives us everlasting life.

Are we part of Jesus and part of his Father? Have we trusted him for our eternal life?

[Discover more about having eternal life in 1 John 1:2, 2:25, 3:15, 5:11, and 5:13, as well as 5:20.]

DAY 30: NO IDOLS
1 JOHN 5:21

Dear children, keep yourselves from idols. (1 John 5:21)

After John writes a fitting conclusion to his letter in 1 John 5:18–20, he tacks on one more verse. He simply tells his audience to keep themselves from idols.

I imagine John finishing his letter and then reading it. He gets to the end and realizes he forgot to address idols. But for him to insert this extra content into the right place in his letter would require rewriting the entire thing. So, he takes the practical step and tacks it onto the end.

But this doesn't make John's warning against

idol worship an afterthought. It's a critical issue for his audience of the day, as well as for us now.

Idolatry is the worship of idols. A second understanding defines idolatry as excessive devotion to something.

Though today few of us would bow down before an idol or struggle with the issue of eating idol-sacrificed meat, our world today excels in excessive devotions—many of them.

These excessive devotions become our present-day idols. Here are some common considerations:

Work

Though we must work to earn money to support our families, our jobs are not the goal, but the means to the end. Yet many people hold an excessive devotion to their work. Placing too much emphasis on our jobs is a present-day form of idol worship.

Money

Too many people view income and their bank balance as a measure of success. More is better.

How much more? They see no upper limit. Though we need money to live, we shouldn't live for money —or let it become our idol.

Possessions

Our materialistic society has an insatiable desire for more. Too often we buy things because we want them, not because we need them. We desire newer, bigger, and better. We covet what our neighbors have. This materialistic mindset of buying and owning things can become our idol.

Hobbies

A hobby is a non-work activity we pursue for enjoyment or self-fulfillment. The best hobbies align our passions and interests with ways to advance God's kingdom or give him glory. Hobbies kept in balance produce personal benefits. Yet we can pursue many hobbies with an excess zeal which threatens to become our idol.

Leisure Activities

In our self-induced, stress-filled life, we need a respite from the busy lifestyle we've created. Though needed for our mental wellbeing, we must guard against filling our non-work time with a frenzy of pursuits. We must seek recreation to draw us toward God, not pull us away. Otherwise, it becomes our idol.

Family

Yes, an excessive devotion to family can become an idol, albeit a well-intended one. Too many parents embrace a child-first focus that rises above everything else. The result is making our family's wellbeing our idol.

Though we would never physically bow down to an idol and worship it, we run the risk of worshiping its modern-day equivalents. Idols were clear in John's day. The issue is much murkier now and may be an even bigger threat to us than it was two thousand years ago.

Let us cast aside all our idols and put God first in everything.

What idols do we struggle with today? What changes must we make in our practices and attitudes?

[Discover more about idolatry in 1 Corinthians 10:14–21.]

JOHN'S SECOND LETTER

John writes a letter to the elect, the chosen lady, along with her kids. Some people assume John uses this intimate metaphor to refer to the church (the chosen lady) and its members (her children). But this interpretation falls apart because the New Testament considers the people as the church, not as two separate parts.

Rather, a literal understanding is that the chosen lady is an actual person. John's note is one of encouragement and instruction to someone he cares for deeply. Because the Bible preserves his letter for us, we can vicariously receive this same reassurance and teaching.

The chosen lady is a faithful follower of Jesus. Let's read on to learn what John tells her.

In what ways has God chosen us? Do our actions align with being chosen?

[Discover others chosen in Acts 9:15, Romans 16:13, Colossians 3:12, and 1 Peter 2:9. Read about *the* chosen one in Luke 9:35 and John 1:34.]

DAY 31: GRACE, MERCY, AND PEACE
2 JOHN 1:1–3

Grace, mercy and peace from God the Father and from Jesus Christ, the Father's Son, will be with us in truth and love.
(2 John 1:3)

John opens his letter calling himself simply "the elder." Though he could have used more prestigious labels, such as "one of Jesus's twelve disciples" or "the one Jesus loved," he chooses the humbler label of "elder."

After his concise two-word phrase to describe himself, he launches into a wordy greeting—one consistent with his poetic style—to his recipients: the chosen lady *and* her children, loved in truth.

(We'll cover John's use of *truth* in tomorrow's reading.) His salutation takes up two verses.

Addressing his audience, he goes on to declare a blessing for them—and himself. This blessing proclaims grace, mercy, and peace from Father God and his Son, Jesus the Christ.

Many people struggle to discern between grace and mercy. Some dictionaries even use one word to describe the other, yet we'll make a distinction between them.

Grace

As it relates to God and us, we understand grace as a divine favor extended by him—our Sovereign Lord—to us as his chosen people. He offers grace to us and extends grace to us.

A simple, yet helpful, understanding is that God's grace toward us gives us good things that we don't deserve.

The word *grace* appears throughout the Bible but most often in the New Testament. In this way we see God's grace coming to us through Jesus.

Mercy

In contrast to grace, mercy is a compassionate treatment from someone in authority—with God as our supreme ruler—to a lesser person. Other examples of mercy include being kind, forgiving, and providing relief from distress.

Our simple understanding of mercy is that God's mercy to us removes the bad things we deserve. Though our sins call for punishment, through God's mercy, given by Jesus, we receive forgiveness.

Mercy is both an Old Testament and a New Testament idea, appearing in over half of the books in the Bible.

Peace

The third element of our blessing is peace. The word *peace* appears in most books of the Bible, showing up around as often as grace and mercy combined.

We often think of peace as an absence of conflict or a freedom from strife. Peace can also be an inner serenity or contentment.

We can embrace John's blessing of peace to

address both these understandings. The first peace is physical and applies to our time on earth. The second peace is spiritual, starting now and extending into eternity.

In this way we can receive God's grace and mercy as ushering in an everlasting peace.

How well do we do at receiving grace, mercy, and peace from God? How can we better show grace, mercy, and peace to others?

[Discover another biblical writer who proclaims grace, mercy, and peace in 1 Timothy 1:2 and 2 Timothy 1:2.]

DAY 32: WALK IN THE TRUTH
2 JOHN 1:4

It has given me great joy to find some of your children walking in the truth. (2 John 1:4)

Truth is a recurring theme in John's writing. He addresses it in twenty-three verses in his biography of Jesus, the gospel of John. The word appears more there than in any other book in the Bible. In second place is 1 John, with ten verses. Third John has five more, with four verses about truth here in 2 John.

John is a champion of the truth.

In his writing, he talks about us knowing the truth, living in the truth, and belonging to the truth. He wants the truth to be in us. And the truth can set us free. We can work in the truth and walk in the truth, just as some of the children of the chosen lady.

But what does John mean when he talks about the truth?

Since John writes with a poetic flair, we'll do best to interpret these passages as more lyrical than literal. In this way, the truth emerges as the message of the good news about Jesus, of him being the way to salvation and eternal life—all themes we've covered. And it's not a stretch to see Jesus as person-ifying the truth—or as the truth personified in Jesus.

With Jesus as the truth, when we follow him, we walk in the truth—just as some of the chosen lady's children.

For her part, the chosen lady, no doubt, desires to pass her faith on to her kids. She's a good mom, one who does her best to raise her children well. As a result, some of her kids live God-honoring lives.

They walk in the truth. But not all do. Some pick up her legacy. Others do not.

She has done what she can to raise her kids right, but how they decide to live their lives is up to them. John affirms her actions, but he doesn't hold her accountable for results outside her control.

Whether we are parents of biological children

or spiritual children, we need to do our best to raise our offspring well. Though we can't control which path our kids take, we can—and should—point them in the right direction.

What can we do to be a better parent to our children and those God brings into our lives? When have we taken on needless guilt for what happens outside our control?

[Discover more about parenting in Deuteronomy 11:19, Proverbs 22:6, Ephesians 6:4, and 1 Timothy 1:18–19.]

DAY 33: WALK IN LOVE
2 JOHN 1:5–6

As you have heard from the beginning, his command is that you walk in love. (2 John 1:6)

I n John's second letter, he continues to repeat themes from his first one. He tells the lady chosen by God the same things he writes to his first audience.

This is not a new command he gives her, but an old one. It's a command given from the beginning: to love one another. And in love, we obey Jesus's commands. The chief one is to walk in love.

We've already covered love at length, addressing it in over half of our readings. Here are the primary messages about love:

We don't need to repeat these lessons here, but we can consider 1 Corinthians 13, the Bible's go-to chapter about love.

The world often uses the word *love* incorrectly and practices it wrongly. We can't love a thing or an activity. We can only love God and love others. Paul gives us a most helpful list of characteristics of how to walk in love.

Love:

- is patient
- is kind
- is not envious
- is not boastful
- is not proud
- is not rude
- is not self-seeking

- is not easily angered
- forgets the mistakes of others
- does not delight in evil
- rejoices with the truth
- protects
- trusts
- hopes
- perseveres
- never fails

When we live out this list, we love one another as John (and others) command us to do.

What must we change to love according to what the Bible says? How can we better walk in love?

[Discover more about loving others in Romans 13:8 and Galatians 5:14.]

DAY 34: BEWARE THE DECEIVERS
2 JOHN 1:7–9

Watch out that you do not lose what we have worked for, but that you may be rewarded fully. (2 John 1:8)

J ohn moves from his encouragement to walk in love to a warning about being on alert for deceivers, whom he calls antichrists (see Day 10). These deceivers share one particular trait that makes them easy to spot. They don't acknowledge that Jesus came to earth as a flesh-and-blood man (1 John 4:2).

This isn't a trivial distinction but an essential one. It's the core tenet of our faith. Here's why:

If Jesus didn't come to earth, we don't have his teaching to guide us, his invitation to follow him, and his sacrificial death to save us and give us eternal life. In the process, we lose the grace his love gives and the mercy his death provides. Along with that, we risk losing his peace (see Day 31).

By denying that Jesus came to earth, these deceivers remove Jesus from Christianity. This is why John calls them antichrists. They are anti-Christ or against Christ (1 John 2:22).

If we remove Jesus from our faith, we lose the uniqueness of Christianity and make it no different than any other religion. This leaves us with something we must do, rather than something we can receive. It means working to earn our salvation instead of accepting Jesus's gift at no cost (Ephesians 2:8–9 and Revelation 22:17).

John worries that his dear friend might fall victim to their deception. He warns her to watch out for them, to stand guard and protect her faith. Though her salvation is not at stake, her eternal reward is. Under their misguided teaching, she could lose part of her reward and not receive it fully. John desires that she receive her full reward.

He states the situation most clearly. If someone gets sidetracked in their faith and doesn't continue to embrace Jesus's teaching, that person doesn't have God in their life.

Yet everyone who continues to abide in Jesus's teaching has both Father God and his Son. They will receive their full reward.

Who might we need to stop listening to because they don't acknowledge that Jesus came to earth in the flesh? What ways might we be in danger of losing our full reward?

[Discover more about God's reward in Matthew 5:11–12, Matthew 6:1–6, Ephesians 6:7–8, Hebrews 10:35, and Revelation 22:12.]

DAY 35: WICKED WORK
2 JOHN 1:10–13

Anyone who welcomes them shares in their wicked work.
(2 John 1:11)

B uilding upon his instruction about the deceivers—the antichrists—John warns the chosen lady to not welcome anyone who holds to their teaching and to not show them hospitality. If she does, she aligns herself with their misguided ways and shares in their guilt of denying Jesus.

John's teaching refers to those who don't acknowledge Jesus's humanity, of him coming to earth as a person. To extend John's command to apply to other types of teaching—such as what we may disagree with or find distasteful—is an over-stretch; it takes his words out of context.

Therefore, this isn't a call to scrutinize the theology of other followers of Jesus, accepting those who align with us and rejecting those who understand faith differently.

Unfortunately, Jesus's church has done just that over the past two millennia, splitting theological hairs over beliefs to decide who's in and who's out. This divides Jesus's church in the process and has resulted in over 41,000 Protestant denominations. Often, these factions mistrust each other, do not welcome each other, and don't get along with each other.

Instead, Jesus prayed that we would be one, just as he and the Father are one (John 17:20–21). Despite our contrary actions, there is one church, and Jesus wants us to be unified in him and through him.

John's teaching doesn't run counter to the unity Jesus wants. Instead, John gives one unique situation for us to watch out for.

This is to be alert for people who don't acknowledge that Jesus came to earth. We should have nothing to do with them, but this doesn't cause division in Jesus's church. If they deny Jesus's saving work, they aren't part of his church to begin with (1 John 2:19). They oppose Jesus and try to take others with them.

If someone denies Jesus, don't associate with them. Otherwise seek the unity Jesus prayed for.

When have we made wrong theological distinctions that caused division in Jesus's church? What can we do to work toward the unity Jesus prayed for?

[Discover more about unity in 1 Corinthians 12:12–13, Ephesians 1:7–10, Ephesians 4:3, and Colossians 3:14.]

BONUS CONTENT: MORE TO WRITE

I hope to visit you and talk with you face to face, so that our joy may be complete. (2 John 1:12)

John wraps up his letter with a heartfelt statement of his desire to meet with the chosen lady, the dear lady, face to face. John ends his third letter, this one to Gaius, with a parallel sentiment (3 John 1:13–14).

In both cases John says he has more to say. But instead of writing it in a letter, he wants to visit them both and tell them in person.

We don't know if John is able to meet either of these two people and tell them the rest of his message. If he doesn't, then his letters to them are the extent of his communication, which is all we are privy to as well.

Because John opted to not put the rest of his message in his letters, we don't know what else he wanted to say—and it's possible his recipients didn't either.

Though I'm not being critical of John's decision, I do see this as an encouragement to not put off important communication for later. Later may not happen. If we have something to write or say, we should do it now and not delay.

Communication over a distance was hard in John's day, but we have many faster and easier options now. We should use them and not jeopardize our message being lost or delayed.

What do we need to say that we've been putting off?

[Discover more in 3 John 1:13–14.]

JOHN'S THIRD LETTER

John's letter to Gaius is a short one. It's a warm note, full of encouragement and affirmation. John also reinforces some teachings with Gaius. The Bible preserves this letter for us to read in 3 John.

This is likely the same Gaius grabbed by the riotous crowd in Ephesus. He, along with Aristarchus, travels with Paul to tell others about Jesus (Acts 19:29). This makes Gaius a missionary.

We also know that Paul baptized Gaius (1 Corinthians 1:14).

We get one more insight into Gaius as Paul wraps up his book to the Romans. He notes that Gaius sends greetings to the Roman followers of Jesus, making mention of Gaius's hospitality

(Romans 16:23), a trait we will see repeated in 3 John.

Paul has enjoyed Gaius's hospitable nature and so has the whole church. We don't know where Gaius lives, but it could be in Derbe (Acts 20:4). Regardless, the hospitality of Gaius is well known in the area.

Gaius first travels as a missionary and later opens his home to other missionaries as they travel to tell others about Jesus.

May we follow his example.

Are we known for our hospitality? If not, what should we do about it?

[Discover more about hospitality in Romans 12:13, Hebrews 13:2, and 1 Peter 4:9.]

DAY 36: WALKING IN THE TRUTH
3 JOHN 1:1–4

I have no greater joy than to hear that my children are walking in the truth. (3 John 1:4)

J ohn's third letter is to his dear friend Gaius, a man John loves in the truth. *Loving in the truth* is the same affirmation he writes to the chosen lady in his second letter, 2 John.

It thrills John to hear the testimony of others that Gaius is faithful to the truth and continues to walk in it. John has no greater joy than to know that his children are walking in the truth.

If this idea of walking in the truth sounds familiar, it's because John uses the same language to affirm some of the chosen lady's children who are walking in the truth (Day 32).

Though it should no longer surprise us, only John's letters mention this idea of *walking in the truth*. The rest of the Bible doesn't use this phrase, so we can't tap its other appearances in Scripture to understand it better.

Even so, we've talked about how John's use of *truth* is a nod to the good news about Jesus and the eternal life he offers, with truth personified in Jesus.

Though Jesus never tells his followers to "walk in the truth," he often invites them to "follow me." Even though he sometimes tells people to do other things, the simplest instruction he gives is "follow me." When we follow Jesus, we stop doing what we're doing, thereby changing our course (we repent) to follow him.

Therefore, when we decide to follow Jesus, we decide to walk in the truth. As such, John's euphemism to *walk in the truth* is synonymous with Jesus's invitation to *follow me*.

Though *walking in the truth* starts with a one-time decision to follow Jesus, it's also ongoing. *Walking* is active. We must build on our initial commitment to our Savior by making an intentional decision each day to continue to walk with him. In this way we find ourselves continuing to follow him. As we do, we walk in the truth. And this delights John, with unsurpassed joy.

May we live lives of walking in the truth each day.

How well are we doing at walking in the truth? What actions should we take today to continue to follow Jesus?

[Discover more about following Jesus in Luke 9:23 and John 10:27.]

DAY 37: FAITHFUL SERVICE TO MISSIONS

3 JOHN 1:5–8

Dear friend, you are faithful in what you are doing for the brothers and sisters. (3 John 1:5)

John opens his letter to Gaius by affirming his faithfulness to the truth and his continuing to walk in it (3 John 1:3). Now John likewise affirms Gaius's faithfulness in his service to the brothers and sisters.

What is this service?

Quite simply Gaius shows love to missionaries. Though strangers to him, he cares for these traveling ambassadors of Jesus, showing them hospitality and implicitly providing financial support. In doing so, he works in tandem with those mission-aries for the truth, that is, for Jesus.

Gaius spent time as a missionary, traveling with Paul. Though he no longer does this, he still has a heart for missions. Through him we see multiple ways to help others learn about Jesus, either directly or indirectly.

Serve as a Missionary

As we've already covered, Gaius travels for a time with Paul on a missionary journey. Though Paul takes the lead, Gaius does his part in telling others about Jesus. He even faces persecution for his efforts.

Jesus tells his followers to go throughout the world and tell everyone about him (Mark 16:15). Yet not even Paul spends all his time doing this. He has seasons of traveling as a missionary and seasons of staying home. Likewise, Gaius goes out for a time and stays home for a time. This doesn't diminish his commitment to Jesus's call. It just takes a different form.

Welcome Missionaries

As missionaries travel through Gaius's area, he provides them with a place to stay, showing them love and offering hospitality. Though his role is indirect, it's an essential act of support, enabling the missionaries to be more effective.

Financially Support Missionaries

Since missionaries seldom receive monetary support from the people they're serving, they need help from others. John calls for their support and we can infer Gaius sets an example in doing so, taking a leading role.

Pray for Missionaries

Though not mentioned in this passage, we can also pray for missionaries. If Gaius welcomes and gives to missionaries, it's safe to assume he also prays for their work. Paul models this when he asks the churches for prayers on his behalf as he proclaims the good news of Jesus (Ephesians 6:19–20 and Colossians 4:3–4).

As John tells Gaius, these all work together for the singular goal of spreading the truth of Jesus.

Though we may not go throughout the world to tell others about Jesus, how can we work with those who do? What missionary can we support?

[Discover more about being a missionary for Jesus in Matthew 28:19–20, Luke 24:48–49, and Acts 1:8.]

DAY 38: SELFISH DIOTREPHES
3 JOHN 1:9–10

I wrote to the church, but Diotrephes, who loves to be first, will not welcome us. (3 John 1:9)

After affirming and encouraging Gaius, John changes the topic. He mentions two men. They are in sharp contrast to each other. The first gives an example to avoid, while the second shows an example to follow.

These two men are Diotrephes and Demetrius.

First up is Diotrephes. This is the only time he shows up in the Bible, so we don't know his background or anything else about him, except what John shares in his letter to Gaius, which is most insightful.

In short, Diotrephes has issues. Lots of them.

To start with, this guy loves to be first. He has a huge ego, with a me-first mentality. He wants to be in charge and insists everyone listen to him and follow him. No one can tell him what to do, not even the revered apostle John.

At one time, John wrote a letter to the local church Diotrephes is part of. We don't know which church this is. And we don't have the letter to read. Regardless, the arrogant Diotrephes refused to accept what John said. He dismissed John's authority, rejected his teaching, and declined to welcome him.

On John's next visit he promises to publicly call out Diotrephes's inappropriate actions.

In addition to loving to be first and not accepting John's authority, Diotrephes compounds the problem by gossiping about John and other disciples. Diotrephes's smear campaign spreads damaging rumors. He must stop.

In addition to Diotrephes's refusal to welcome John and his team, he also refuses to welcome other believers when they visit. This is in sharp contrast to the laudable actions of the hospitable Gaius.

But this isn't only a personal attack on John and an assault on his leadership. Diotrephes also stops others in the church from welcoming visitors. And he expels them from their local gathering if they do.

Diotrephes is part of Jesus's church, but his actions don't honor Jesus or support his followers. Diotrephes serves as internal opposition to Jesus. He is in the church, but he works against her.

May we never do that.

When do we seek to be in control or want to be first? What do we need to change to honor Jesus and better support his church?

[Discover more about being first in Matthew 19:30 and Mark 9:35.]

DAY 39: ESTEEMED DEMETRIUS
3 JOHN 1:11–12

Demetrius is well spoken of by everyone—and even by the truth itself. (3 John 1:12)

After cautioning Gaius about Diotrephes, John instructs Gaius to not imitate evil but what is good. Given the context, with this following the warning about Diotrephes, we realize that John is calling Diotrephes evil. Before we temper this label of evil by saying Diotrephes isn't evil, merely his actions are, read what else John says. Anyone who does evil doesn't know God.

In contrast, John tells Gaius to imitate what is

good. Anyone who does good is from God. This leads us into the testimony of Demetrius.

There are two men named Demetrius in the Bible. The first is Demetrius, the silversmith, whom Luke writes about because he opposes Paul and the followers of Jesus (Acts 19:23–41).

John, however, writes about a different Demetrius. This Demetrius is one held in high esteem. He shows up in John's letter to his dear friend Gaius.

Gaius may know Demetrius, or John may anticipate that the two of them will one day meet. Of Demetrius, John simply writes, everyone speaks well of him—even the truth itself. This mention of the truth is John's poetic nod to Jesus and his good news of salvation. It's important to John that Gaius know this.

Imagine that. Jesus speaks well of Demetrius. May we live worthy lives that bring about the same affirmation from our Savior.

Though he doesn't need to add to Jesus's testimony of Demetrius, John does anyway. He tacks on that *we*—that is, he and his team—also speak highly of him, and we don't lie.

We don't know why John feels it's important to communicate this truth about Demetrius to Gaius

—or warn him about Diotrephes. Perhaps both accounts jointly serve to encourage Gaius to continue his hospitality, being esteemed like Demetrius, and not swayed by the evil actions and threats of people like Diotrephes.

Even more so, we're left to guess why Demetrius is so well esteemed. He must be a man of noble character and impeccable integrity. In this regard, may we all be like him.

Demetrius's God-honoring character provides an example for us to emulate. For when others speak well of us, we can best represent Jesus to them.

Do people speak well of us? What might Jesus say about us?

[Discover more about another man God speaks well of in Hebrews 11:4.]

DAY 40: PEACE TO YOU
3 JOHN 1:13–14

Peace to you. (3 John 1:14)

J ohn ends his first letter with an abrupt instruction to keep away from idols. In contrast, he wraps up his next two letters with a smoother, more intimate farewell. To both recipients he expresses his desire to see them in person and tell them more, face to face (see Day 35: Bonus Content).

In his second letter, to the lady chosen by God, John adds greetings from the children of her sister —who is also chosen by God. These would be her nieces and nephews.

In John's third letter, he again sends greetings and encourages Gaius to likewise greet the friends there. John also simply proclaims a blessing of "Peace to you."

We've already talked about peace in Day 31. There we noted that *peace* occurs throughout the Old and New Testaments. It's ironic, however, that *peace* occurs in every New Testament book *except* 1 John.

First John aside, let's look at what else John writes about peace.

Peace occurs five times in the gospel of John, each instance coming from the mouth of Jesus. Our Savior declares peace to us and wants us to experience his peace. This is so affirming.

The first time, just before his betrayal and arrest, he gives his disciples some final instructions. In this address, Jesus says, "Peace I leave with you; my peace I give you." This isn't a worldly peace but a spiritual one. Therefore they —and we, along with them—shouldn't worry or fear (John 14:27).

Next, after telling the disciples what is about to happen, Jesus says, "I have told you these things, so that in me you may have peace." Though the world will cause trouble for them—and us—take heart, for Jesus has overcome the world (John 16:33). This is a reason to feel his peace.

For the last three times *peace* occurs, Jesus says the same thing. This happens after he rises from the dead and meets his disciples in resurrected form. He twice tells them as a group, "Peace be with you!" (John 20:19, 21). Then he commissions them to tell others about him.

But Thomas isn't there. Jesus later appears to him with the same greeting, "Peace be with you!" (John 20:26).

Let's also consider John's epic revelation. As John opens the record of his vision, he addresses it to the seven churches, with the words "Grace and peace to you from him who is, and who was, and who is to come" (Revelation 1:4).

May we have the peace that Jesus and John proclaim.

Do we have Jesus's peace in us? Do others notice his peace in our lives?

[Discover more about peace in Luke 2:14, Acts 10:36, Romans 5:1, and Galatians 5:22–23.]

If you liked *Love One Another,* please leave a review online. Your review will help others discover this book and encourage them to read it too. Thank you.

WHAT BOOK DO YOU WANT TO READ NEXT?

onsider these other books in the 40-Day Bible Study Series:

- Dear Theophilus (the Gospel of Luke, formerly That You May Know)
- Dear Theophilus, Acts (formerly Tongues of Fire)
- Dear Theophilus, Isaiah (formerly For Unto Us)
- Dear Theophilus, Minor Prophets (formerly Return to Me)
- Dear Theophilus, Job (formerly I Hope in Him)
- Living Water (the Gospel of John)

- Love Is Patient (Paul's letters to the Corinthians)
- A New Heaven and a New Earth (John's Revelation)
- Run with Perseverance (the book of Hebrews)

FOR SMALL GROUPS, SUNDAY SCHOOL, AND CLASSROOMS

L*ove One Another* makes an ideal eight-week Bible study discussion guide for small groups, Sunday School, and classrooms. In preparation for the conversation, read one chapter of this book each weekday, Monday through Friday.

- Week 1: read 1 through 5.
- Week 2: read 6 through 10.
- Week 3: read 11 through 15.
- Week 4: read 16 through 20.
- Week 5: read 21 through 25.
- Week 6: read 26 through 30.
- Week 7: read 31 through 35.
- Week 8: read 36 through 40.

When you get together, discuss the questions at the end of each chapter. The leader can use all the questions to guide this discussion or pick which ones to focus on.

Before beginning the discussion, pray as a group. Ask for Holy Spirit insight and clarity.

As you consider each chapter's questions:

- Look for how this can grow your understanding of the Bible.
- Evaluate how this can expand your faith perspective.
- Consider what you need to change in how you live your lives.
- End by asking God to help apply what you've learned.

May God bless you as your read and study his word.

IF YOU'RE NEW TO THE BIBLE

Each entry in this book contains Bible references. These can guide you if you want to learn more. If you're not familiar with the Bible, here's a brief overview to get you started, give some context, and minimize confusion.

First, the Bible is a collection of works written by various authors over several centuries. Think of the Bible as a diverse anthology of godly communication. It contains historical accounts, poetry, songs, letters of instruction and encouragement, messages from God sent through his representatives, and prophecies.

Most versions of the Bible have sixty-six books grouped into two sections: The Old Testament and the New Testament. The Old Testament contains thirty-nine books that precede and anticipate Jesus. The New Testament includes twenty-seven books and covers Jesus's life and the work of his followers.

The reference notations in the Bible, such as Romans 3:23, are analogous to line numbers in a Shakespearean play. They serve as a study aid. Since the Bible is much longer and more complex than a play, its reference notations are more involved.

As already mentioned, the Bible is an amalgam of books, or sections, such as Genesis, Psalms, John, Acts, or 1 Peter. These are the names given to them, over time, based on the piece's author, audience, or purpose.

In the 1200s, each book was divided into chapters, such as Acts 2 or Psalm 23. In the 1500s, the chapters were further subdivided into verses, such as John 3:16. Let's use this as an example.

The name of the book (John) appears first, followed by the chapter number (3), a colon, and then the verse number (16). Sometimes called a chapter-verse reference notation, this helps people quickly find a specific text regardless of their version of the Bible.

Although the goal was to place these chapter and verse divisions at logical breaks, they sometimes seem arbitrary. Therefore, it's a good practice to read what precedes and follows each passage you're studying since the text before or after it may contain relevant insight into the portion you're exploring.

Here's how to look up a specific passage in the Bible based on its reference: Most Bibles contain a table of contents, which gives the page number for the beginning of each book. Start there. Locate the book you want to read, and turn to that page. Then flip forward to the chapter you want. Last, skim that chapter to locate the specific verse.

If you want to read online, enter the reference into BibleGateway.com or BibleHub.com. Also check out the YouVersion app.

Learn more about the greatest book ever written at ABibleADay.com, which provides a Bible blog, summaries of the books of the Bible, a dictionary of Bible terms, Bible reading plans, and other resources.

ABOUT PETER DEHAAN

Peter DeHaan, PhD, wants to change the world one word at a time. His books and blog posts discuss God, the Bible, and church, geared toward spiritual seekers and church dropouts. Many people feel church has let them down, and Peter seeks to encourage them as they search for a place to belong.

But he's not afraid to ask tough questions or make religious people squirm. He's not trying to be provocative. Instead, he seeks truth, even if it makes people uncomfortable. Peter urges Christians to push past the status quo and reexamine how they practice their faith in every part of their lives.

Peter earned his doctorate, awarded with high distinction, from Trinity College of the Bible and

Theological Seminary. He lives with his wife in beautiful Southwest Michigan and wrangles crossword puzzles in his spare time.

A lifelong student of Scripture, Peter wrote the 1,000-page website ABibleADay.com to encourage people to explore the Bible, the greatest book ever written. His popular blog, at PeterDeHaan.com, addresses biblical Christianity to build a faith that matters.

Read his blog, receive his newsletter, and learn more at PeterDeHaan.com.

BOOKS BY PETER DEHAAN

For the latest list of all Peter's books, go to PeterDeHaan.com/books.

40-Day Bible Study Series:

Dear Theophilus (the Gospel of Luke, formerly That You May Know)

Dear Theophilus, Acts (formerly Tongues of Fire)

Dear Theophilus, Isaiah (formerly For Unto Us)

Dear Theophilus, Minor Prophets (formerly Return to Me)

Dear Theophilus, Job (formerly I Hope in Him)

Living Water (the Gospel of John)

Love Is Patient (Paul's letters to the Corinthians)

A New Heaven and a New Earth (John's Revelation)

Love One Another (John's letters)

Run with Perseverance (the book of Hebrews)

Holiday Celebration Bible Study Series:

The Advent of Jesus (an Advent devotional)

The Ministry of Jesus (an Ordinary Time devotional)

The Passion of Jesus (a Lenten devotional)

The Victory of Jesus (an Easter devotional)

Bible Character Sketches Series:

Women of the Bible

The Friends and Foes of Jesus

Old Testament Sinners and Saints

More Old Testament Sinners and Saints

Visiting Churches Series:

Shopping for Church

Visiting Online Church

52 Churches

The 52 Churches Workbook

More Than 52 Churches

The More Than 52 Churches Workbook

Other Books:

Jesus's Broken Church

Martin Luther's 95 Theses

The Christian Church's LGBTQ Failure

Bridging the Sacred-Secular Divide

Beyond Psalm 150

How Big Is Your Tent?